An Introduction to Bernard Lonergan

Peter Beer

Note: While the text remains the same as in the 2009 edition, footnotes of this 2020 edition, sometimes enlarged, now refer to recent published volumes of the completed set of the *Collected Works of Bernard Lonergan*.

Published in Australia by Sid Harta Publishers Pty Ltd,
ABN: 46 119 415 842
23 Stirling Crescent, Glen Waverley, Victoria 3150 Australia
Telephone: +61 3 9560 9920, Facsimile: +61 3 9545 1742
E-mail: author@sidharta.com.au

First published in Australia 2009
This edition published 2020
Copyright © Peter Beer 2009, 2020
Cover design, typesetting: Chameleon Print Design

The right of Peter Beer to be identified as the Author of the Work has been asserted in accordance with the Copyright, Designs and Patents Act 1988.

By permission of Oxford University Press for excerpts from *"Later Christian Fathers"* edited by Bettenson H (1970)

By permission of the University of Toronto Press for excerpts from *"The Collected Works of Bernard Lonergan"* (1988f)

Beer, Peter
An Introduction to Bernard Lonergan
ISBN: 978-1-925707-36-6
pp230

About the Author

Peter Beer SJ is Director of the Lonergan Centre, Canisius College, Pymble, Sydney, New South Wales. He joined the Jesuit Order, graduated in arts at Melbourne University, was ordained to the priesthood and pursued doctoral studies at the Catholic University of America in Washington, graduating in 1972.

He was awarded a travelling scholarship for postgraduate research at the Lonergan Center at Regis College, Toronto, in 1974–75 where he studied Lonergan's seminal works, *Insight* and *Method in theology*. After teaching at the diocesan seminary in Melbourne, in 1976 he was appointed to the Union Theological Institute of the Sydney College of Divinity, where he taught systematic theology and methodology until 1998. He has published a number of articles applying Lonergan's transcendental method.

In 1979, he invited Professor Frederick Crowe, of Regis College, on a lecture tour to the Australian capital cities. After this successful tour, he invited others to join with him in setting up a Lonergan workshop that meets regularly for the presentation of papers and discussion.

Contents

Analytical table of contents

Preface

This book aims to help form a basis for inquiry into Lonergan's achievement (a mid twentieth century Canadian philosopher and theologian) in his new approach to the great philosophical questions: what do I do when I know something? (cognitional theory), why is doing that knowing? (epistemology) and what do I know when I do that? (metaphysics).

Lonergan deals with these questions somewhat more deeply in his major works, *Insight* (1957, 1992) and *Method in theology* (1972, 2017). Here he invites one to discover in oneself the dynamic structure of one's own cognitional and moral being, and in doing this, one finds an operative procedure that is not open to radical revision. In fact, Lonergan has unearthed a dynamic conscious framework for creativity, a method that grounds all investigation that is intelligent and critical. It is a resource that is transcendental in that it is the concrete and dynamic unfolding of human attentiveness, intelligence, reasonableness and responsibility, and this unfolding occurs whenever one uses one's mind in an appropriate fashion. This method for investigators, too, is new in its finding eight tasks that are distinct and separable stages in the single process from data to results. This method can be adapted to any subject in which investigations are responding to past history and are to influence future history.

Acknowledgements

I remember with gratitude my doctoral mentor Dean Carl Peter of the Catholic University of America, Washington DC. I dedicate this book to Professor Frederick Crowe SJ of Regis College of the University of Toronto who introduced me to Lonergan's *Insight*. I thank especially Professor Tom Daly SJ of Jesuit Theological College, Melbourne, and also Professor Michael Vertin of St Michael's College of the University of Toronto, lifelong friends and mentors in Lonergan Studies. I appreciate the advice and criticism of Professor Daniel Monsour of Regis College and Professor Matthew Ogilvie of the University of Dallas in my writing of this book. I am grateful too to my Australian Jesuit Provincial, Mark Raper, for allowing me time to write this work.

I thank also Annette Hansen for her invaluable and expert editing.

Finally, I dedicate this book to the memory of my beloved parents Charles and Mary Eva Catherine Beer. I remember with gratitude the help of my sister Patricia and especially of my brother John who has supported my work and Australian Lonergan Research. I mention with gratitude my early education at the Presentation School, Murwillumbah, and secondary education at St.Ignatius College at Riverview, Sydney. I wish to mention with appreciation also my former Marist Professorial Colleagues and the students of the Union Theological Institute of the Sydney College of Divinity.

Introduction

This book wishes to offer but a simple and very brief introduction. It aims to enable the reader to secure for herself or himself a solid foothold or something of a base camp from which to set out to achieve a comprehensive understanding of human knowing and deciding and of the search for what is intelligible, true and of value. This book, as a starting point, finds a helpful illustration of cognitional structure, operative in Hitchcock's *Dial M for Murder*. Successive references to facets of the unfolding plot with diagram upon diagram, incrementally aim to reveal something of the self-assembling elements of the conscious formal dynamic structure of knowing. Something similar to a dendritic pattern forms as an image for grasping knowing's self-assembling levels of conscious intentionality. Thus an increasing enlightenment reaches a highpoint in the diagram of sublation present in knowing's structural elements in Chapter 2.

Certain essential elements of Lonergan's transcendental method will be noted. One will be led to identify one's interior cognitional activities by their technical terminology and defined function. One will be drawn to note the transcendental notions that initiate the respective levels of conscious intentional inquiry. One will be helped to note transcendental precepts that regulate the sublating procedure of this inquiry. One will also be led to recognize the relevance of intellectual, moral and religious conversions that also pertain to critical realism that is fully expounded in Lonergan's *Insight* (1957, 1992) and *Method in theology*[1] 2017 (1972,2017). Critical realism is then proposed to enable one to recognize the misapprehensions issuing from the prevalence of naïve realism, empiricism, and idealism.

It is to be hoped that at the end of this book, one will begin to prize the command and liberation that critical realism brings and the ready discernment of positions that fit in with keeping to transcendental method, as distinct from counter-positions that bypass that method.

So, chapter one notes the knowing process operating in the investigation of Chief Inspector Hubbard. Chapter two defines more clearly the elements of this knowing process, the interdependence of the consciousness of data and the occurrence of insight, and the consequent formulation of ideas and hypotheses, and the verification of the latter and the values attained so that knowing and valuing can be clearly outlined.

Chapter three inquires into the nature of objectivity. Chapter four continues this investigation into the source of objectivity and the relation of human knowing to being and reality. Also will be noted the worlds mediated by meaning and motivated by value that arise from the human desiring to know.

Chapter five then uncovers the need for appropriate stances to be achieved in order to know and to value objectively. Chapter six offers an historical example where the appropriate intellectual stance of realism emerged through vigorous, early conciliar debate.

Chapter Seven offers a brief insight into investigative method developed out of critical realism, available for all manner of research into data in order to arrive at ultimate results.

---

1   B.Lonergan, *Insight*, 1957; 2nd ed., 1992, (875pages), CWL3; and *Method in Theology*, 1972; 2nd ed., 2017, (CWL 14).

N.B. In these footnotes, reference is made to this volume, *Method in Theology* 2017(CWL 14), moreso than to A Third Collection, 2017,(CWL 16).

Prologue

A statement of the evidence for a metaphysics has to be in dynamic terms. If a spatial image and a military metaphor may be helpful, the advance of metaphysical evidence is at once a breakthrough, an envelopment and a confinement. The breakthrough is effected in one's affirmation of oneself as empirically, intelligently and rationally conscious. The envelopment is effected through the protean notion of being as whatever one intelligently grasps and reasonably affirms. The confinement is effected through the dialectical opposition of twofold notions of the real, of knowing and of objectivity so that every attempt to escape is blocked by the awareness that one would be merely substituting some counter-position for a known position, merely deserting the being that can be intelligently grasped and reasonably affirmed, merely distorting the consciousness that is not only empirical but also intelligent and not only intelligent but also reasonable[2].

---

2   B.Lonergan, 1992, pp.508-509

7

Chapter 1

Chief Inspector Hubbard's spirit of inquiry in Hitchcock's *Dial M for murder*

At times, we will refer to the detective story, *Dial M for murder*, filmed by Alfred Hitchcock. It would be difficult to follow these references unless one has seen the film, readily available on DVD. It is not the brilliant attempted assassination scene that is pivotal for our interest; it is the final scene. In darkness, all are waiting inside in silence. All eyes are focused upon the brass lock of the door to the apartment. This scene will be a constant refrain in our inquiry. Hitchcock, in the dimly lit room, focuses a strong beam of light upon the shiny brass doorlock, for all the drama hinges on that lock. The moment a key is inserted and is able to turn, the denouement can begin. Then Hitchcock suddenly allows us to hear slowly the first and second and further clicks of a key turning in that lock!

After the trial of Mrs Wendice and her conviction for murder, Chief Inspector Hubbard still had what he found to be relevant questions that had not been answered. Early on, a line of information put to him by evidence that the husband had malevolently construed had led the Inspector to the possibility of the wife's guilt. Later, upon correction of this line of information, new evidence enabled the Inspector to find new questions requiring answers and these brought him to outlay a new idea

9

on what had really happened. This new possibility the Inspector formulated into an hypothesis.

This new theory cast into serious doubt that the wife, though already condemned at the Old Bailey, was guilty after all. Because he had yet to find answers to the last relevant questions that would prove her innocence and would instead prove the husband's guilt, he therefore could not and would not say that the wife was innocent or guilty. Inspector Hubbard just could not bring himself to say something was true and real unless it could stand up to his persistent questioning.

As the Inspector noted down answers to the many different questions he was asking, we notice how varied they are. Is there arising a pattern to his questionings? Does this pattern lead him to know the truth he wants so desperately? And how reliable is this pattern that emerges[3]?

Stages of Chief Inspector Hubbard's inquiry

1.1   Different sets of data were presented for the Inspector's attention

When the Inspector first appeared at the doorway of the Wendices' apartment, he found, unbeknownst to him, the living room somewhat rearranged after the husband, Mr Wendice, had tampered with the evidence. Earlier, the husband had done this after he had sent his wife into the bedroom to rest after her ordeal in being attacked. Indeed, it had been an ordeal for her as she had struggled valiantly, stabbing the assassin with her sewing scissors. (Hitchcock presents this so dramatically and with a subtle touch of humour!)

Though we in the audience might well see how Mr Wendice

---

3   Cf.B.Lonergan, 2017, p.10, par 4; p.11, par.1

was framing his wife, whose money he could not live without, the carefully inquiring Inspector, as he noted meticulously each piece of pertinent data, could not but follow the trail constructed by the husband. This was a path that implied that the man who was stabbed was blackmailing Mrs Wendice over a love letter her lover, the detective story writer Mr Halliday, had written to her. Mr Wendice, in rearranging the scene of Swan's death, had planted this letter in the pocket of Swan, the victim who lay stretched out on the floor with the scissors in his back.

So, already, different sets of relevant data are being presented for one's attention. The first set of data belonged to the actual chain of events. Here, as planned with Swan, Mr Wendice had rung Mrs Wendice around 11 pm to get her up and out of the bedroom next to the living room and to come into the living room where she stood behind the writing desk to answer the phone. Wendice knew it was his wife's custom to always answer the phone from that position, where she would stand in front of the living room curtain and face away looking over the desk out into the living room. He had planned for Swan to be waiting there so Swan could emerge unnoticed from the curtain behind and strangle her.

Things happened almost as planned, but instead of Swan strangling Mrs Wendice, it was she who brought *him* down. She put up a mighty struggle in which she was able to reach for her rather large pair of sewing scissors and plunge them, with a touch of Hitchcock grandeur, into the back of Mr Swan. Mr Swan then fell onto the floor in such a way as to secure the entry of the scissors to the hilt, into his back, killing him.

Swan had used Mrs Wendice's key to gain entry into the apartment. Wendice had stolen this key from his wife's purse and had left it under the staircase carpet outside the apartment for Swan to gain entry into the Wendices' living room where Swan would wait behind the curtain near the desk.

Mr Wendice had already paid Swan a third of his commission for murdering his wife.

1.2 The newly disposed data of tampered evidence led the Inspector to an understanding of the wife's guilt

But a different set of data was provided for Inspector Hubbard on his arrival. This new set of data resulted from Wendice interfering with the first set. The new train of data he constructed was disposed to facilitate the Inspector towards understanding a possible chain of events where the wife appeared to have let in to the apartment the man whom she seemed to have cause to eliminate as a source of blackmail.

The husband had told his wife not to ring anyone, including the police, and not to touch anything till he got there, and when he returned to the apartment, he sent his wife to rest on the bed in the bedroom. He then got to work redisposing the data – to reset evidence. He took out of his own pocket and put into the dead man's pocket the love letter to his wife from her lover, Mr Halliday. It was then evident that it was Wendice who had stolen this letter from his wife's handbag at Victoria Station.

The letter, as Mrs Wendice had told Halliday, had been missing from its usual place in the bag that was later mysteriously recovered. Mrs Wendice had not been able to burn this particular letter from Halliday who must have written with especial endearment to her. Also, a year ago, when Halliday was visiting London, Wendice had followed his wife to an assignation she had had with Mr Halliday. 'They looked so natural together', Wendice had said in his preparatory, conspiratorial meeting with Swan. In that meeting, Wendice had let Swan pick up the letter of Halliday's to Mrs Wendice so Swan would be leaving his fingerprints on the letter, as if he had had the letter and was holding it to blackmail Mrs

Wendice. Furthermore, the husband found the scarf his wife had said the would-be assassin had used to try to strangle her with. It was a scarf Swan had had in his pocket and had tied around Mrs Wendice's throat in the struggle. Wendice had then put this scarf – a leading piece of evidence towards a valid defence Mrs Wendice could make – on the log fire in the living room.

Of course, the attention of the Inspector was turned to receiving the data of evidence presented to him as he entered the room, and so Inspector Hubbard could not help but find this love letter from Halliday to Mrs Wendice in the pocket of the dead man lying on the floor. This letter found on Swan, and with Swan's fingerprints on it, could lead one to suspect the probability of Swan blackmailing Mrs Wendice. Also, the Inspector could not find the scarf Mrs Wendice had said the dead man had used to try to strangle her.

Doing as her husband had told her, Mrs Wendice did not answer truthfully to the Inspector as to why she had not immediately called the police, nor did she tell the Inspector that her husband had told her *not* to call the police. Her husband had asked her to lie about this and she, trusting her husband, had lied to the Inspector about it.

So, the Inspector, little by little, was being led to grasp the intelligible organization of the line of data, as construed by Mr Wendice, that hinted at this – namely, that Mrs Wendice had not been truthful, was not to be trusted and was acting suspiciously. In fact, the data presented hinted that Mrs Wendice was having great trouble with this apparent blackmailer, and it also seemed quite probable that she had planned to kill him. Added to this was the data on her affair with Halliday, and this lost her the sympathy of the jury.

Indeed, all the data as thereby presented and understood enabled the idea of her guilt to be clearly formulated at the ensuing trial at the Old Bailey. This idea, which the husband's malevolently disposed data had very much occasioned, was formed into an hypothesis of her being guilty of murdering a supposed blackmailer. The hypothesis the jury found to be proven and verdict was pronounced accordingly. Mrs Wendice was to be hanged, to be carried out without much delay.

1.3 After the trial, the Inspector became aware of some unanswered relevant questions that for him demanded answers

The Inspector had found that Wendice and his wife, very early on, had made wills naming each other as the beneficiary. At the trial, much had been made of Mrs Wendice's affair with Halliday, and the strength of their love revealed in the letter found on Swan proved this. The Inspector could now gain new insight into the course of events, formulating an idea where the husband Wendice, not wishing to be left penniless when his wife might leave him, could have been guilty of seeking to secure his wife's money. Wendice, the Inspector now realized, might well not wish to let slip his only chance to gain a large fortune.

Mr Halliday was presently revisiting London after a year's absence, and this visit could well end in Mrs Wendice leaving her husband for Halliday. So, Wendice possibly could have been planning to secure his wife's fortune on the eventuality of Halliday's return. Wendice may have long arranged to set in motion, at the right time, a scheme to have his wife murdered. The occasion could have been when he, in apparent friendliness with Halliday, took him out to dinner. Dining with Halliday, he would have an alibi while he could have arranged Swan to act as an assassin and have his wife murdered.

On the strength of this new understanding of the added data, Inspector Hubbard set about constructing his new hypothesis that would account for and reorganize intelligibly all the data gathered both before the trial and since Mrs Wendice's condemnation.

After the trial, there had unexpectedly arisen suspicious behaviour on the part of the husband. Where did Wendice get the rather large amount of money he was spending from the time of his wife's arrest? Two further questions were also relevant for the Inspector – they gnawed at him somewhat. Why was there no key found in the dead man Swan's pocket? The Inspector said men usually carry around a key to their residence. And also, why did the key in Mrs Wendice's purse not open her apartment door? Where was Mrs Wendice's key, the one of only two keys that opened the Wendices' apartment door? In fact, the Inspector had come to find that the key in Mrs Wendice's purse was not her key, which was missing, but Swan's key. How then did his key get into Mrs Wendice's purse?

The Inspector, saying he had to go to Scotland, asked Wendice to pick up some effects at the police station, including Mrs Wendice's handbag. In the meantime the Inspector, who had a coat almost identical to that of Wendice's, had managed to switch coats, gaining Wendice's own key to the apartment, the only other key, apart from Mrs Wendice's key that was still missing. The Inspector had intended to run a test to see if Wendice knew of his wife's key being under the carpet on the staircase outside the apartment. The Inspector, as if by mistake taking Mr Wendice's coat, left the apartment. Wendice later also left. But the Inspector, who had been waiting for Wendice to leave, returned to the apartment and, to gain entry, used Wendice's key that he had taken from Wendice's coat. The Inspector could then set rolling his experiment to test Wendice.

Chief Inspector Hubbard had two final questions yet to be answered. Did the wife know of the key being there under the staircase carpet? There had to be eliminated the possibility of Mrs Wendice having left her key outside under the carpet. Then finally, the most important question of the whole drama: did the husband know of his wife's key being there under the staircase carpet? This would mean that he had stolen his wife's key to leave outside for Swan to use to gain entry to kill Mrs Wendice. He could not leave his own key there because, to create an alibi for the time of the attempted assassination, he had to use his own key on his apparently innocent return from dining out with Halliday.

1.4 The Inspector's insight that completed the coherent understanding of his new hypothesis explained all the data prior to and following the trial

The Inspector now grasped the insight, the possibility, that Wendice conspired with Swan that he would secretly leave his wife's key for Swan to use to get into the apartment to murder her. Afterwards, Swan, Wendice reminded him, was not to forget to put the key back where he had found it. And with this final piece of organization of the intelligible pattern of this new hypothesis, Inspector Hubbard gained an answer to this question as to why Swan's own latchkey was not in his pocket but in fact was in Mrs Wendice's purse. The Inspector now grasped the possibility that Wendice, on rearranging the data of the murder scene before the police arrived while his wife was resting in the bedroom, had taken the key in Swan's pocket that he thought was Mrs Wendice's key and put this – Swan's own latchkey – into her purse.

Wendice's mistake was that he did not think of Swan replacing the key under the staircase carpet upon his immediate use of it before he entered the apartment. Instead, Wendice thought Swan would be intending to replace the key as he left the apartment after he had killed Mrs Wendice. Brillantly, the Inspector now grasped the possibility that Swan had replaced the key *before* he entered the apartment.

This insight of the Inspector finally set up the coherence of the new hypothesis. The new insight put everything into an

understandable or intelligible arrangement to explain the killing.
Everything that had happened before and after the trial now had
its intelligible place; the insight unified all the data of evidence
and intelligently organized everything. But a coherence is only a
possibility; it has yet to be proven! The condition that linked the
hypothesis with fact would truly be fulfilled with the concrete
experiential element of Wendice opening that door with his wife's
missing key. It would *then* be evident Wendice had conspired to
leave his wife's key there for the assassin to use. So, it would be
evident that the master criminal would be Wendice himself and
not his wife. They would then know everything. It was also an
insight that gave considerable excitement to the Inspector.

It is helpful to note, that in the tenth chapter of his major work
Insight, Lonergan explains that concrete judgments of fact rest on
invulnerable insights. These insights grasp that further pertinent relevant questions do not in fact arise. One can get beyond probability
and indeed reach certainty. One can make a judgment of fact that is
correct beyond reasonable doubt. One cannot expect to rely upon
it being impossible that further pertinent questions could not arise.
Lonergan shows that interpreting literally and applying rigorously
universal doubt rests on flawed cognitional theory. Of course, our
very brief introduction of Lonergan's enormous achievement can
aim but to offer some salient direction of his thought being published in twenty or so volumes by the University Press of Toronto.

1.5 But the Inspector found that his hypothesis being proven depended upon two final relevant questions being answered

Two questions remained to be answered in order that the
Inspector's new hypothesis could be proven. Did Mrs Wendice
know of the key being there under the staircase carpet? If so,

his hypothesis would fail to isolate the possibility of it being unquestionably the husband as having placed the key there. And if she did not know of the key being there under the staircase carpet, then the most relevant question was finally to be met: did Mr Wendice know of its being there? If this were the case, the Inspector's hypothesis would stand. It would meet the conditions set for it to no longer be assented to as a mere possible course of events; instead, the Inspector's hypothesis would be assented to by any reasonable person as being fact.

So, there were two experiments the Inspector had to carry out. First, he had Mrs Wendice brought from prison to go to her apartment to use the key in her purse. The key, as the Inspector had discovered, was Swan's own apartment key and of course could not open the door, and Mrs Wendice, the condemned woman, genuinely could not explain why what she thought to be *her* key in *her* purse could not open the door. The Inspector then realized Mrs Wendice was innocent of implication of any dealing with Swan.

1.6 The final relevant question being answered fulfilled the conditions for the Inspector to give his assent to the hypothesis.

Mr Wendice, when he happened to return, took the key from the raincoat he had and could not open his front door. He then looked at the coat's tag, found this coat happened to belong to the Inspector (the Inspector had switched coats) and then thought his own coat, with the key, was on its way to Scotland with the Inspector. He remembered being told that his wife's handbag was at the police station. It would have his wife's key, he thought. He had told Swan not to forget to replace that key under the carpet on the staircase outside as he was leaving the apartment, and Wendice had gauged that Swan, being killed, was prevented

from doing this. So, when redisposing the evidence, Wendice
thought it was his wife's key that he had secretly retrieved from
Swan's pocket and put into his wife's purse.

Wendice returned from the police station with his wife's
purse and found that the key from her purse did not open the
door. We could see Wendice, who was puzzled, slowly walking
to leave the building. The Inspector was watching this too from
a window in the apartment. Wendice was wondering: why was
this not his wife's key? What could Swan have done with it? 'Yes,'
the Inspector said, 'he's got it!'

The insight must have come to Wendice: Swan must have
put it back under the carpet *before* he entered the apartment. If
Wendice had the only key in Swan's pocket and he had put it into
Mrs Wendice's purse – and this was the key, yet it could not open
the apartment door – then the key he, Wendice, was holding in
his hand, most probably was Swan's own latchkey. So, Wendice
suddenly understood that Mrs Wendice's key would still be there
under the staircase carpet.

Wendice turned and hurried back to look under the carpet
where he had left his wife's key for Swan, and found the key. He
then opened the door and, to his shock, found all inside the door
waiting for him.

Wendice, without saying anything, caught on immediately
that the game was up and understood too that those standing
there inside, waiting for him, also knew it. Wendice tried to make
a run for it, but a tall London policeman was waiting outside the
door for him. So, Wendice turned back into the apartment and
poured himself a Scotch, saying, 'You must admit, it very nearly
worked!'

Inspector Hubbard's procedure

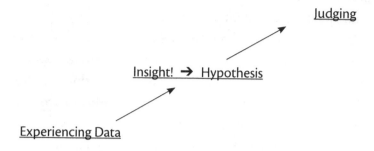

Judging

Insight! → Hypothesis

Experiencing Data

Inspector Hubbard's procedure explained

Testing new idea of hypothesis
till all answers are in →

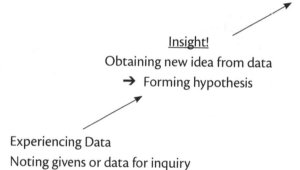

Reflective Insight that
conditions are met to
proceed to judging the
idea to be true or not true!

Insight!
Obtaining new idea from data
→ Forming hypothesis

Experiencing Data
Noting givens or data for inquiry

1.7   In the Inspector's mind, distinct and irreducible mental activities were at work that conspired in proper order for him to reach the judgement that solved the murder case[4]

    1.7a   Chief Inspector Hubbard first attended meticulously to data being presented for his notice

He is very attentive to the data being presented to him as he walks around the room and speaks to people there. Also, he is conscious of his being attentive, for a person speaking just outside his hearing might be saying something pertinent that could be of interest to his investigation. He is not questioning if he is being attentive, yet he is aware if his attentiveness has been hindered.

    1.7b   The Inspector's native human spirit of wonder, his spirit of inquiry, issued forth in successive sets of questions

Chief Inspector Hubbard is very much aware of wanting to understand. His wanting to understand focuses upon pieces of information pertinent to the killing of the now dead man on the floor of the Wendices' apartment. Then he wanted to know how all the pieces of information he was getting fitted into some plausible explanation of how the man was killed.

---

4   Cf.B.Lonergan, 1988 (CWL 4) "Cognitional Structure" pp.206–208: a neat summary of the many different activities, their relationship and their unity in the process of knowing; Cf. Also B. Lonergan, 2017, *Method in Theology*, (CWL 14), p.10, par.4

However, he would not be satisfied with how things could *possibly* fit together; he wanted also to know *if in fact* things *did* come together as thought to give a true explanation as to why the man was killed. These two sets of questions – namely, questions asked in order to understand why and how the killing might take place, and then questions for reflection on that very understanding in order to verify that things did truly happen that way are entirely different. One set seeks possibility, the second set seeks fact. We see this twofold desire, to understand and to know for sure, began to be operative in the Inspector as he started to assemble data for questioning.

He noted first the names of those who were 'of interest'. He also noted times and places. He was working on level one of intentional consciousness; that is, firstly, he was wanting and intending to gather all the pertinent data for questioning for his criminal inquiry.

His wanting to know then took him further to a second type or level of inquiring by putting questions – such as what, why and how – to the data gathered. He asked how these pieces of data fitted together into a plausible explanation. He would then formulate an hypothesis that would offer a possible reason as to why the killing occurred.

With this explanation reached, he put forward questions of a third type or a higher level, but was the explanation correct? He became conscious of conditions for verifying the explanation. Those conditions had to be met before he could pronounce the explanation he had reached to be the true one. So, we observe in the Inspector a driving power; firstly, to begin to notice what was provided by the crime scene; secondly, as the Inspector gathered more data, he began to ask why and how? What sense is it all making? So, he questions that assembled data in order to grasp a possible understanding. Thirdly, he raised the questioning to a new level of inquiry i.e. he reflects on this hypothesis offering an understanding of the chain of events that is a true possibility by checking the possible hypothesis against the relevant sense data, checking and asking: is there sufficient evidence coming in to support what is proposed as a possible explanation for the killing?

Again, the drive the Inspector experienced caused different sets of questions to be raised. As he became aware of what people were reporting to him, there was simultaneously active in his consciousness a drive from a native human spirit of wonder and inquiry. This spirit of wonder was asking what, how, why in regards to data coming in from what he saw, heard and noticed. He was diligent in inspecting all the visible effects of the struggle of Mrs Wendice with her would-be assassin. He carefully listened to all that was said. He was quick to perceive Mrs Wendice's hesitation over answering his questions.

This attentiveness to such things occurred on the basic first level of his consciousness. It was succeeded by the spirit of wondering and questioning that pertained to the Inspector's second level of consciousness. This second level was the level of strictly intelligent activity beyond the activity of the senses. Sense activity was nonetheless needed as providing data for that intelligent questioning: what did all this data mean?

So, accompanying this presentation of data, the Inspector became conscious of questions such as: What motive could the killer have had? How did the killing happen? What sense can be made of all this data being presented for my attention in this room? Again, the Inspector is asking: is there some linking up, some pattern that is understandable (intelligible) in this line and succession of data being presented to my awareness? That is, the Inspector was consciously driven to find a genuine possible solution as to why or how the man came to be there, stabbed in the back. He was then to express this possible solution in an adequate hypothesis.

A new line of questioning then arose. The Inspector was aware that upon reflection over all the relevant data, he had to progress to such a point where he could arrive at understanding that the conditions had been fulfilled for him to assent to the hypothesis proposed to explain the killing. Such fulfilment would consist of nothing less than answering the final relevant question to be raised in regard to verifying the hypothesis. Only then could he know for certain who the guilty person was.

We know now that this native spirit of wondering was the prior and enveloping drive that took the Inspector from sensing and imagining to understanding and on to judging correctly. This correct judgement was named 'knowing'. This desire to understand issuing forth during the course of respective subsequent questionings – first for intelligence (what, how and why?) and secondly for judgement (but is this idea correct? verified?) – prevented the Inspector from being content merely with *perceptions* of the flow of outer and inner experience.

Lonergan says: 'The desire to know, then, is simply the inquiring and critical spirit of man': 'inquiring' (seeking to understand – level 2 of intentional consciousness) and 'critical' (questioning for judging – level 3 of intentional consciousness). The desire to know is different from all other desire. It is named 'pure desire'. You cannot compare it with other desiring, but it is to be known 'by giving free rein to intelligent and rational consciousness'. This pure desire is powerful and pulls one up from 'perception and conation, instinct and habit, doing and enjoying'. So, the desire is cool, detached, disinterested, not out for satisfying the one recounting the events; the desire's objective is to know what is to be known.

This desire gets one interested in solving problems. It keeps one from being satisfied with a lack of answers. It makes one give assent to what has its conditions met. It is a desire for content and for what is to be known, and for what is known as fact. It scorns the satisfaction of mistaken understanding and prizes correct understanding, not because it gives satisfaction but 'because its content is correct'. For the pure desire to know is the root of all that can be affirmed, of all that can be understood and conceived. Its objective includes all that is known and all that remains to be known[5].

In summary; firstly, the Inspector was noticing a dead man lying there, along with the scissors that killed him, but the Inspector was doing more than just noticing all these data. With Lonergan's helpful explanation of the pure desire to know put in explanatory terms, we can give this account of the Inspector's inquiring activity.

Secondly, the Inspector was asking how did all of what he found there, through his own observation and from what he was told, make sense? Why was there a dead man there? What did the death of this man, killed in this way, possibly mean? Could the Inspector discover an intelligible pattern in all the data being provided to his consciousness? How could he tie together all the data presented to him, or unify all this data in some organized way to make sense of it? The Inspector was desiring insight! A new and fresh act of understanding, an intelligible unity of all this data, assembled for him. All these questions were for intelligence and understanding!

---

5   "It is a desire to know. As mere desire, it is for the satisfaction of acts of knowing, understanding...But as pure desire...it is not for cognitional acts and the satisfaction they give their subject, but for cognitional contents, for what is to be known.' Lonergan, 1992,p.373,pars. 2-3

Then, thirdly, he was aware he wanted more! He wanted to know as fact what really went on in regards to the dead man found in this apartment. He was not only intelligent but critical too; he wanted to understand, but he also wanted to judge if he had understood correctly!

In the procedures of Inspector Hubbard's mind, we can discern a basic pattern of cognitional operations that is at work in every cognitional enterprize. For that reason, the pattern can be called 'transcendental' – a transcendental method.

Transcendental method

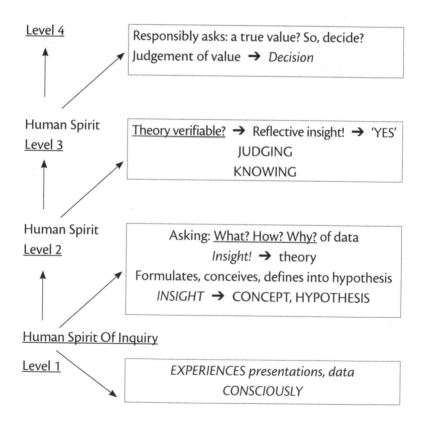

1.7c   Chief Inspector Hubbard gained new understanding or Insight!

Now we come to focus upon the fundamental activity that Lonergan found so radically significant. We will introduce Lonergan's technical terms as we proceed.

The Inspector does not know that the husband has been orchestrating the presentation of data. Wendice has redisposed the data to hint at a possibility that implicates Mrs Wendice. So, the Inspector is led to catch on to this possibility, to gain a new understanding or insight as to what all the data before him adds up to. He intelligently and freshly ties all the data together at a point.

His tying of all the data as an organized whole suddenly makes sense of it all. Matter, as parts spread out, could only organize itself in a material juxtapositioning way into a collection of disorganized parts put beside one another higgledy-piggledy, but an insight unifies and organizes data in an intelligible order and gives understanding.

The understanding prompted by the arrangement of clues laid by the husband is something new added to the data presented, for the clues themselves do not say that Mrs Wendice may have done away with the man on the floor with the scissors in his back, nor is this tying together done simply by taking a material image of parts outside of parts. True, data that can be imaged by our senses are needed, for one cannot tie together either what our senses do not happen to receive disparately or what our senses do not sense at all.

Again, insight is not material activity; this tying together is beyond what matter can do, for matter of itself cannot organize, being made up of parts outside of parts that exist side by side temporally or spatially. As such, these side by side parts need to be tied together in some order that makes sense. Any material may merely cover parts but without duly explaining the parts and their arrangement. Thus, the tying together is an organizational function that intelligence adds. It enables data to be tied together and organized according to a certain pattern that can answer the questions: What is this? How is this so? Why is this so? That is, these questions aim to find an intelligible pattern that gives understanding of something.

The fresh activity of understanding, however, that Inspector Hubbard suddenly has can unify the parts, organising all parts intelligibly. For example, Inspector Hubbard noticed Wendice spending money liberally after Mrs Wendice's trial. Questions followed in the mind of the Inspector. Where did he get this money? Why was no key found in Swan's pocket? Whose key was it in Mrs Wendice's purse and where was Mrs Wendice's key? Did Swan forget, or did he put the key back before he entered the room? etc. After so many questions, the Inspector got the new insight that Swan had put the key back before he entered the apartment to kill Mrs Wendice. This new insight was certainly not the mere placement of any piece or pieces of data randomly side by side. Rather the new insight was unifying and organising and making sense of the data of those answers since the trial. This unifying of these ideas was done by a non-material power acting beyond the capability of material spread out randomly.

But to grasp what an insight is, one has to be very attentive to what is actually happening as one suddenly catches on to something. As one sets about solving a problem, often one finds oneself sketching out something and reworking this sketch, trying to make it come out. Suddenly, one has grasped a possible way in which all the pieces fit; a pattern emerges that unifies and organizes the data to make sense. (For specific treatment of insight in algebra, arithmetic, art, science and in other contexts, see Lonergan's work, *Insight*[6].)

Upon getting his new insight, the Inspector was clarifying the idea by spelling out the content of the insight in a concept. This concept expressed the data as organized and understood by the Inspector's insight. He was conceiving the possibility that his insight had caught hold of i.e. that Swan was blackmailing Mrs Wendice and that she had lured her blackmailer there and deliberately killed him.

So, in gaining insight, the Inspector had grasped something he could not see or hear with his senses, for he had suddenly immaterially attained how all that data was held at a point, how it all fitted together, understandably unified. In obtaining insight, he was aware of something new, a new activity, but it was not seeing a new image or just receiving a sense datum; instead, he could grasp how all that sense data unified and fitted an understandable, non-visible pattern. He conceived or conceptualized this intelligible pattern into a theory on why the man was killed. No amount of data or merely gaping or looking at the data could have produced that theory. Obtaining insight is in no way a mere *looking* at something; it includes this but adds so much more.

This intelligible oneness achieved by the application of insight would need an accompanying image. This image ('phantasm' as

---

6   "To have an insight… is not peculiarly difficult, it does require 1. The authenticity that is ready to get down to the elements of a subject, 2. Close attention to instances of one's own understanding and, equally, one's failing to understand, and, 3. Equally, the repeated use of personal experiments in which, first, one is genuinely puzzled and then catches on." B.Lonergan, 1988,p.209,par.1; also cf. Daly, Thomas V, SJ. (1991) Learning from Lonergan at Eleven, Method: Journal of Lonergan Studies 9(1), pp.44-62

Aquinas called it) would provide data that was thus understood or unified (the concept) by the insight. Again, there could not have been added an act of unifying data if there had not been present the data to be understood. Without data, the additional unifying application of insight would have been lost.

Take another example, given so clearly by Professor T Daly: a joke is getting to the point quickly; the punchline. The elements of the story are being presented as data not yet organized, not yet making sense – disparate. Then the punchline – and lo! All the elements suddenly unify. The punchline holds them all at a point, unified, unexpectedly making sense.

(We will not blame Professor Daly for the following example.) One was asked, 'What do they call a man who murders in a wheat field?' A pause ensued, then a solution was offered: 'A cereal killer!' It is not just looking at the elements so far – the wheat field, the killer, the murdered person etc. – that makes you laugh. No, it is something new. Your immaterial power is now suddenly unifying the temporally and spatially spread out events and images. It is a unification of all the stages of the joke's elements together at a point that has been building up. And so, insight is 'getting the point'. Here in the joke, insight happens suddenly and unexpectedly, intelligibly unifying at a point all those stages built up, and this causes excitement[7].

1.8   Insight is neither intuition nor perception

Insight is not intuition. Intuition is a 'seeing' of what is immediately provided through some experience or impression, without

---

7   Cf. B.Lonergan, 1992, p.29, par.1"What better symbol could one find for this obscure, exigent, imperious drive(to know) than a man naked, (Archimedes) running excitedly, crying "I've got it"?"

questioning for either understanding or judgement. Intuition does not result from questioning what, how or why, nor from asking: is it so? Intuition is *not* understanding or judgement.

As an example, one comes home one day with an intuition that things are not right in the house and finds the house has been ransacked. One may have some experience of smells, of images, or of a feeling, and this experience may arouse puzzlement as well as dispose data to provide clues for an insight to occur. But beyond these clues, an intelligible unification of data could not occur. For insight to occur, a sufficient actual set of pertinent data has to be presented for intelligent unification and intelligible organization. Intuition may still be but an imagination. Having an intuition, one has not yet had a sufficiently clear answer as to what, how, or why something possibly happened.

Also, intuiting may be but experiencing an image immediately. What is obtained by intuition is unquestioned, unintelligible and uncritical, or just imagined or visualized, perhaps in some dream. There could not have been, without clear concept and sufficient reason, any adequate reflective grasp of what concretely did happen. Intuition, then, is what is immediately provided through some experience, without questioning for either understanding or judgement[8].

---

8   Where 'intuition' according to Scotus grasps what is already existing and present, "Insight" Lonergan says, merely grasps what might be relevant and is to be affirmed only if verified. Cf. B.Lonergan 1988, p288, note 'p'. Also, "Interpretation is not a matter of looking at signs" Lonergan says, for he rejects the "principle of the empty head…where all one has to do is to look at a text and see what is there". He asks, "in fact, what is out there? There is just a series of signs. Anything over and above a re-issue of the same signs in the same order he says, will be mediated by the experience, intelligence, and the judgement

Nor is a perception an insight! Interests and preoccupations also support perceptions. We also distinguish the interest of scientific investigation from that of ordinary, concrete living. In living, we learn from the past to deal with the present and ready ourselves for future situations. 'Thus the flow of sensations, as completed by memories and prolonged by imaginative acts of anticipation, become the flow of perceptions. It is of the latter perceptual flow that we are conscious'. But when acting in science, we bring sensations into a new context and we let interests, desires and fears of ordinary living slip into the background. The detached and disinterested demands of inquiring intelligence take over; you just keep your mind on your experiment! Imagination will still act but only to bear on a scientific issue. 'Like the artist, the expert in any field acquires a spontaneous perceptiveness lacking in other men, so too does the scientific observer (acquire such spontaneity)'.

What guides the scientist is the *orientation* of the inquiring intelligence that is a pure, detached, disinterested desire, simply, to know. Without this desire, no question would arise, no wonder would arise. So, this desire to know has to dominate, reinforce or inhibit tendencies, excluding other tendencies, so that his percepts move into coincidence with what is named the data of sense. It is then by rigorous training that the scientist masters the difficult art of scientific observation[9].

So, one's mind is first active as it is taking in data; that is, as it notices things provided for one's attention by one's memory, or from what is being presented to one's senses, or from one's

---

of the interpreter....". cf. B.Lonergan, 2017, p.149, par.4. Also, intuition is a mere impression, something unquestioned, unverified, unsubstantiated. In sharp contrast is the attending to all relevant data, and gaining insight and verifying that insight.

9   Cf. B. Lonergan, 1992, p.97, par.2

noticing given circumstances and things. For example, what things came to the Inspector's expert observation as he entered the apartment? He noticed the body of a man with a pair of scissors in his back. On looking into the pockets of the man, there was found the love letter from Mr Halliday to Mrs Wendice, but the Inspector could not find the scarf that, as Mrs Wendice had asserted, the dead man had used to try to strangle her (Mr Wendice had already burnt it).

On noticing this rearranged data, there was a moment when Inspector Hubbard began to catch on, to find a hint and then to grasp the possibility that the wife could have wanted to get rid of the victim, who seemed to be her blackmailer, so that soon, we noticed the Inspector suddenly, unexpectedly (as she seemed such an unlikely murderer) grasp this possibility.

Much later, after the trial, he became conscious of having a new understanding that in fact unified and tied together all the data he had attended to into a whole that did make sense to him. The point was very nearly missed; it had to be grasped in a new unification of data. So, he came to understand anew a possible scheme as he grasped the insight which was the pivotal point; namely, that Swan had replaced the key before he had entered the apartment. The Inspector was particularly happy to have grasped this new point. He then had to verify this new hypothesis, and on the execution of his second experiment, he did so.

Wendice had entered the room, showing he had known where his wife's missing key was. On this concrete data occasioned by the Inspector's last experiment of Wendice's opening the door and walking in, the Inspector got a new reflective insight that gained for him the understanding that he had met all the conditions to be able to proceed to an exact opposite judgement and affirm Mrs Wendice innocent and her husband instead to be the one who was guilty.

The Inspector could not explain philosophically that he had now gained a reflective insight which was something beyond having mere hints and percepts and hypotheses. That he found this reflective insight was something powerful. He had in fact grasped that the concrete data of Wendice's walking into the room using his wife's missing key answered the final relevant question put and so fulfilled the condition required to satisfy him proceeding with full reason to give his assent to his hypothesis. He now knew that the explanation was a true and real one.

1.9 Insight to concept, understanding brings forth expression of the idea caught on to in insight

Act of understanding/ grasping insight in data ➔	Intelligible unity in data ➔	Intelligible unity as:
	Organized Content of Insight	expressed conceived formulated defined
INSIGHT ➔	IDEA ➔	CONCEPT

An insight, as Lonergan says, grasps an intelligible organization that may or may not be relevant to the data perceived or imagined. With insight goes conception or formulation in which there forms a concept where is put together both the content of the insight, that is, the idea, and as much of the image as is essential for the insight to occur.

The Inspector laboured to express clearly the idea or content gained by the insight into the possible guilt of Mrs Wendice, yet he formulated enough of the data needed for one to gain the insight. Lonergan says that 'conception puts together both the content of

the insight and as much of the image as is essential to the occurrence of the insight'[10]. The concept is insight/understanding as
expressed. The data is now organized, now disposed for a mind
to grasp a possible understanding from that data understood. So,
unless insight has occurred, there can be no concept!

Lonergan relates the example of the scientist listening to a
sermon one Sunday. The scientist suddenly, unexpectedly, in
the course of the sermon, gained an insight into how to solve a
problem that had been puzzling him for two years. Daly points
out clearly the movement from insight to concept in this example
of Lonergan's. The scientist's degree of education, Daly says, his
past experiences, his knowledge of languages etc. were conditions for his gaining insight.

The scientist could hardly wait till the sermon finished. He
rushed home, not wishing to speak to anyone lest he be distracted. This data of his two-year-old problem was now newly
understood, newly organized and, as such, was needed for him
to maintain his insight – and he did not wish another image to
distract and to dislodge that set of newly organized data and so
lose his new insight.

Again, the image accompanying the new insight was data now
being more securely and further organized by his understanding.
Because other images could displace the newly organized image
he had, he spent the afternoon in seclusion writing it out, conceptualising formulae and expressions and drawing diagrams
from the data.

These expressions would not necessarily be the same as what
he might have been thinking of during the sermon at the exact
time he had the insight, for now he would be understanding better (not by any kind of 'looking') the organization that the insight

---

10   Cf, B.Lonergan, 2017, p.14 par.2

had given him. So, he would now be unifying the data better, and expressing more clearly that organization of data, than he had begun to do during the sermon.

The organizational power of insight had also fixated some non-pertinent, peripheral data as well; years later, the scientist could even remember what the sermon was about. Yes, indeed, such was the high degree of the fixating power of this insight that some data of the sermon had come under the insight's organizational power. This data, extraneous to what was necessary for his insight to occur, would have been tied together with his scientific data by the insight.

So, for the rest of the afternoon, Daly says, the scientist did not spend time writing out what he might remember of how things happened, having the insight. Rather, he wrote out in more appropriate words or diagrams or formulae the new unity that he was now understanding of the data from the past two years' research. He did not wish to be disturbed; distraction meant losing that set of images that disposed the data for the insight to occur. He kept focused upon this odd set of images in the imagination in such a way that he could translate that set into clearer words and formulae. By the time he had finished, he had expressed the insight very thoroughly and had formulated a very clear concept of what he had got hold of. The clear concept was the relevant data written out adequately as expressing the insight.

Another person might read what he had written, those formulae etc., and not understand it, for a concept expresses the insight. Without insight, without understanding, such a one would not have the concept even though he had the formulae in front of him. The concept is the data as understood in its unity, achieved by the insight[11].

_____

11   And further, Prof.Daly emphasizes the concept organized by the insight

Another exercise may help. You take up a puzzle of how to join, in four continuous straight lines, nine dots evenly placed in a square. You work at the diagram. You feel boxed in. Then someone may say you are trying with lines being drawn within the limits of the square. This is a hint, a clue which is perhaps the beginning of an insight. If you can take the hint and grasp that you might solve the puzzle by drawing *beyond* the square then you are grasping a possible organization of the data. That is, you have an insight, a non-material grasp of a possibility. It can be that possibility is a key word for helping to pin down what is meant by insight.

But an insight, a possibility, is not the solution. So, let us suggest that you now try with your pen to dispose data differently. You extend the line beyond the limits of the square. After some attempts, you find that you can continue to connect up with other dots. As you draw, the idea, or what you understood in the insight, is becoming more than a possibility; you find you are connecting up all the dots, and you are doing this in four straight lines. In fact, you are verifying your new idea gained in the insight. And as you keep going and finding the dots linking up into four straight lines as required by the puzzle, meeting the conditions of the puzzle and finding fitting, concrete data, your excitement grows. You truly have solved it!

So, then, once you have insight, you have grasped a possibility. Verification is where a possibility is found to truly work, as you

---

as 'data as understood'. And in referring to the circle that Lonergan uses as an example(B.Lonergan, 1992, pp.31-35) where the image of spokes in some equality from a wheel hub thinned out is for disposing data for one to grasp the insight as to why the circle is round: 'equality of spokes' is an image, the words holding it all at a point, and this image then supports the insight's concept of equal, co-planar radii. Then, being systematic, Daly says that to be universally communicable, one uses the terms, 'radius', 'circumference', 'centre', that relate to each other in an intelligible way.

connected all the dots in four straight lines, without lifting pen from paper. You have met all the conditions.

Again, as you reflect back over the conditions of the puzzle set, you note how you got the clue; that you had been confining your drawing to within the square. Almost straight away, you got the direct insight that perhaps it was possible to solve the puzzle by your going *outside* the square, then you do this and proceed to verify your insight by connecting all the dots as required. As you were proceeding to connect the dots, there was a moment where you grasped the insight that you were able to fulfil the conditions set, and so you had to say with some relief and pleasure that you truly had solved the puzzle.

Here you have an example of a direct insight that provides possibility as well as an example of a reflective insight that you have fulfilled the conditions required. This fullness of reason demands you proceed to the judgement of fact.

1.10 Through insight and concept, the Inspector formed an hypothesis

Inspector Hubbard's new direct[12] insight then unified many

---

12   Cf. B. Lonergan, 2017, p.176 par.1. One has a direct insight inasmuch as one 'grasps how things fit together'. As one selects evidence that is formal, not merely potential: namely, those data that relate to one another through an interconnected set of questions and answers; so one assembles a series of insights that interrelate and complement one another, correct one another, and eventually coalesce into a single view of a whole: one gains this direct insight into how things fit together. So then after thus selecting and constructing one gains a reflective inverse insight that something does not fit; but then is able to grasp a direct insight into what is left to stand up to persist questioning: so to grasp a virtually unconditioned—a conditioned whose conditions are fulfilled.

things, events and evidences that were spread out in space and time. They were all data understood and organized intelligibly by that insight. Insight was an exercise of this human spiritual power, of the Inspector's able mind, to understand afresh, to 'catch on', and brought with it its own expressions of what it had caught on *to*. These expressions consisted of understood data presented in their newly organized intelligibility.

The content of Inspector Hubbard's insight, as he was catching on afresh, is called 'the idea he caught on to', and this idea is expressed by the concepts or expressions that convey the intelligibility of the data newly understood by the insight. One can make frequent efforts to put clearly and adequately in apt concepts what one's fresh insight has got hold of.

When you see people struggling to find the right words to express an idea they have got hold of, they are struggling to conceive, to define, to formulate into concepts what the insight got hold of – namely, the idea, the content of the insight. We saw the scientist absorbed in his conceptualising, devoting the afternoon to the effort of finding more adequate formulae to express the content gained by his insight. So, seeking the right word to express the idea of his insight, Inspector Hubbard took care to choose the correct terms. He corrected Halliday by pointing out that though they thought Mrs Wendice was innocent, they did not yet know she was.

So it was then that Inspector Hubbard excitedly came upon the direct insight into why Swan's own latchkey was in Mrs Wendice's purse and why her own key was missing. This insight had led him to satisfactorily complete formulating a new hypothesis.

So one then grasps by this reflective insight that conditions are fulfilled to be able to affirm that the hypothesis does answer the final relevant question for a correct understanding of the data. Cf. B. Lonergan, 2017, p.175, par.4.

The Inspector was then able to construct a sequence of events that could make sense and that would suggest a solid possibility that Mr Wendice had orchestrated a murder attempt upon his wife but that things had not gone according to plan, for Wendice very possibly slipped up on the one point that could have caused his downfall i.e. he may not have happened to think of the assassin, Swan, putting Mrs Wendice's key back under the carpet before he entered the apartment.

With the Inspector grasping this possible lacuna in Wendice's thinking, the Inspector conceived a coherent hypothesis so that his new concept could well turn out to explain how it was a planned assassination attempt that had gone awry and not the cold-blooded murder of a blackmailer. So, Inspector Hubbard's new insight brought intelligible order to all that had happened as it explained how Wendice could have orchestrated the whole event. This explanation seemed to cause everything to fall into place. It was as the Inspector, speaking to Halliday, had said of his test to verify his new theory: 'The moment he (Wendice) walks through that door, we will know everything!'

1.11 Insight, concept, hypothesis and theory yet propose an unverified possibility until the final relevant question is answered

The Inspector knew that his hypothesis was as yet only that – a theory. Mr Halliday had said, 'I know she is innocent!' but Inspector Hubbard corrected Halliday, saying that it was as yet not *known* that she was innocent. The Inspector made it clear to all about him that Mrs Wendice's innocence was not yet something proven as fact beyond a reasonable doubt as long as this final question went unanswered; namely, did the husband know of the key under the staircase carpet? The Inspector was waiting for conclusive evidence that would come only from answering this final relevant question, for its answer would settle everything once and for all as to what had really happened.

How was Inspector Hubbard to find such evidence? He had to set a test, an experiment whereby the husband would have to rely upon his wife's key to get him into the apartment. This need would cause the husband to think over the course of events that had happened to turn out perhaps not completely in the way he had planned them. This reflection might get him to pick up on something he had missed. So, the Inspector conjectured that actual need might bring the husband to ask why this key in Mrs Wendice's purse was not her key to the apartment?

The data of the whole investigation was now understood in a new light brought about by the Inspector's new insight. This insight, expressed by a new conceived hypothesis, would be presented and accepted for verification. This verification would happen if and when Wendice inserted and turned his wife's key in the lock. The intelligible pattern of the Inspector's concept would then be conclusively verified to all inside the apartment! Fully evident, then, would be how the husband had suppressed evidence; for example, his destroying the scarf that the wife had insisted the assassin had used to try and strangle her and how the husband had misleadingly planted his wife's letter on Swan's body in order to incriminate his wife. Then, in addition, the subsequent trial and wife's condemnation and sentencing would be understood anew and correctly. The guilt in the whole affair would be judged anew.

1.12   Inspector Hubbard experienced his spirituality anew the moment he grasped a new type of insight: that he now had fulfilled the rational conditions he needed to proceed to give his interior assent; and indeed he consciously experienced himself under

pain of being irrational to not so proceed and to say
'yes' to what his hypothesis proposed.

Before the Inspector could say he was in fact right, he had to
enter upon a process of verifying his hypothesis. The Inspector
therefore had two experiments arranged, to answer two final
relevant questions respectively.

The penultimate question was: did the wife know of the key
under the carpet? Could she have been in the habit of leaving
the key there? It was a matter of some urgency to have these
answers quickly as she had been convicted and was to be exe-
cuted the next day. The Inspector had informed the Home
Secretary of the unanswered questions that cast all that had
transpired in the criminal case so far into serious doubt, and
the Inspector had been given permission to carry out his two
experiments in order to get to the truth of the matter beyond
a reasonable doubt.

So, the wife was given back her purse, taken from prison, and
told to go into her apartment. When she tried to use the key
in her purse to enter the apartment, she could not understand
why it did not work. It was clear that she in fact did not know
whose key it was that was in her purse. She had no idea that the
key in her purse was Swan's own latchkey. Importantly, she did
not know where her key was. A woman facing the gallows has
no time for games; she did not even attempt to look under the
staircase carpet. She really had no idea it could be there.

It still remained to be seen if the husband knew of the key
being under the staircase carpet outside the apartment, so to set
up the test, the Inspector arranged for the husband to have to
pick up at the police station his wife's purse that contained what
he thought was her key to the apartment

After the prior relevant, penultimate and final questions had been answered, the Inspector was not in the least inclined to say, 'I have not yet enough evidence or relevant questioning answered before I can proceed to give assent and say "yes" to the hypothesis of the husband's guilt.' The Inspector was only too fully aware it would have been silly and irrational of him not to go ahead and to give assent; for instantly, as the door opened with the husband using his wife's missing key to get in, he could not and did not fail to grasp with reflective insight that his hypothesis was correct and that he had fulfilled the conditions for proceeding to give assent. And at the same very moment, he grasped that, reasonably, he had to proceed.

The Inspector, on seeing Wendice open the door with the only key available – Mrs Wendice's missing key hidden under the staircase carpet outside – was instantly aware of his being rationally empowered to proceed to give assent to Wendice being guilty. Though the Inspector had this awareness and acted upon it, he did not thereby know the awareness as such. This awareness was his 'consciousness' at the time.

1.13 Consciousness

1.13a Consciousness is not knowing

The teacher held up a print of Matisse's painting, *The sailor*. The teacher asked what did they, the students, notice, or what were they given as they looked at this picture, what data presented for their attention? Well, for quite a while, observations were offered on the qualities of the painting, on the period of painting to which it belonged, on impressionism and post-impressionism and comment was also offered even on what went on in the mind of the painter etc. Eventually answers dried up – silence! The teacher persisted with the question: 'What else are you given as you look at this painting?' to some annoyance of the members of the class.

This annoyance continued till someone shifted notice to consider the person looking at the painting. 'Well, we have to be looking at the painting.' So, they came to grant that although they did not attend to it being their own activity, it was involved in their one same act of looking at Matisse's *The sailor*. Thus, their own activity was a given in their very same action of their looking directly at the picture.

And then the teacher still persisted: 'Yes, and what else are you given as you look at this painting?'

Now, catching on to the prior answer as a clue, they more quickly came to answer the teacher along these lines: 'Well, we are required to be there doing the action of looking, and we are aware of ourselves while we are doing the looking, though focused upon the painting, and not attending to ourselves being the ones doing the looking. So, we ourselves too are merely but truly a given datum of consciousness as we focus alone on the painting.'

The teacher seized upon this achieved insight and replied to the students: 'So, in the act of looking that you direct towards an object, in that very same act you said you are conscious of the act of looking being *yours*. Also, in that very same act of looking at Matisse, you say, you are conscious of the activity of looking being done by yourselves and also that it is you yourselves who are present, as a given, doing the looking, without yourselves being the object of your attending that is anyway focused on Matisse's painting of the *The sailor!*'

The teacher went on to say: 'Indeed, then, you are conscious of yourselves as subjects doing the action of looking, though you are not putting yourselves as an object of any looking or as an object of any questioning or as an object of any analysis.'

It is then, may we agree with the teacher, that we experience not only our focusing upon the object but also that we experience ourselves as subjects focusing upon or intending the object.

'Again, though,' the teacher continued, 'is this being conscious of ourselves looking an added second action to the actual looking?'

Rather quickly came the reply: 'No, because our being conscious of ourselves was also occurring at the very same time we were giving our whole attention to *The sailor.*'

'So,' the teacher went on, 'you were being aware of yourselves looking. You grant then that as you focused upon Matisse's *The sailor* that both your action of focusing and also your own selves are subjective givens to your consciousness.'

Here we note that the one action is both conscious *and* intentional. As we intend, i.e. hold the object (*The sailor*) in mind or wonder about it, ourselves *and* our looking are simultaneously given or present to our consciousness. As one focuses upon anything, these two – the subject's focusing and the subject herself or himself – are something merely given (as datum), present and not yet questioned, as mere conscious data, unattended to. Again, it is the one act that is intrinsically intentional and intrinsically conscious. So, a subject is present as a subject doing the attending, while an object is present not as attending but as being attended to[13].

Again, the Inspector's very experiencing or being conscious of himself operating is not another operation in addition to the intention that is being experienced. The Inspector's very action of conducting the test is itself intrinsically intentional in regards to the object, but the action is also intrinsically conscious in that he is at the same time aware of himself as the one attending[14].

---

13   B.Lonergan, 2017,p. 12, par.3; also,Lonergan, 1988, pp.208-210

14   CF. B.Lonergan, 2017, p.12, pars.4-6; Also, 1990,pp.15-17; and 1992, pp.344-350

At first, I am aware of my skin being affected as I lie on the beach. I ask, what am I feeling? I attend to the data and can obtain this understanding that I am being stung. I note the data of my skin and the little creature with the long proboscis inserted in my skin. It appears to be a mosquito. This stinging is a content of my consciousness that has been questioned for understanding with the result that I can name it as a mosquito bite. I ask, but is it real or am I imagining it? I check that I am not dreaming but truly feeling stung and am awake. I quickly complete my reflection and would not be so foolish as not to give assent to the fact that I have been bitten.

Again, the original content of my consciousness has been questioned for understanding and for judgement. I objectify this content of my consciousness only as I pay attention to what is affecting my skin and ask the questions: What is it? Is it so? That is, I intend something only as I have something in mind to attend to and to question. Then I seek to understand it and to verify my understanding of it and then I intend to do something about it. Before, I was just conscious of this datum of being stung and had not been attending to it till I directed my attention to it *as it happened*. I instantly began to question this datum, making it the object of my intention to know. I answered through understanding and judgement.

After these questionings and answers, I got to know what before I was only conscious of; namely, that I was being bitten by a mosquito.

And so we come to know then what we are as yet only conscious of. What we have attended to or questioned on the levels of intentionality is then no longer something merely subjective, for it is now held up as an object for questioning, for understanding and verification. It is understood and conceived in order to be assessed if it can stand up to persistent questioning so that it is intended to be known if it is true and real – or not.

It is through experiencing, understanding and judging that we conscious subjects, by intending and questioning, transcend ourselves to affirm that the object of our questioning does exist independently of our thinking, in its absolute realm. So, through our sublating, self-assembling compound of intentional activities – namely, experiencing, understanding and judging – we ourselves are to be known as *knowing, conscious* subjects!

1.13b Consciousness and self-knowing

Now we have noted in Inspector Hubbard those cognitional activities of experiencing, understanding and judgement taking place that brought about his knowing the real person who was responsible for the death of Mr Swan. In observing these activities and in discovering their interaction, we have found a way to follow in order to know the truth of the matter. Further, if we speak exactly, we can name both the activities that take place in coming to know anything and name also their exact definition according to their interrelating functions. That is, we can name theoretical terms, as science comes to name its technical terms.

Inspector Hubbard was conscious all along of himself and of his subjective actions; also as he raised his ultimate question and conducted his experiment to find if Wendice was guilty. That is, all along he was intent and focused upon getting to know if Wendice was guilty. That was his goal in the experiment – nothing else. He was not focusing on himself as the inquiring subject of these actions, yet as he focused upon the object of his inquiry, he was present to himself, or conscious of himself, and of his actions (unquestioned as these were) as data (or 'givens') during his focusing upon Wendice; however, if he was questioning these aforementioned, mere conscious givens, he would be acting objectively in regards to them since he would be directing his attention upon these activities themselves, intending them as the object of his inquiry. They would then no longer be mere givens to his consciousness but themselves also data under questioning for understanding and judging and so also objects for knowing.

In order to get to know the party guilty of the crime committed, we have found that Inspector Hubbard, had to first experience the events of the course of his investigation; and second, understand the events he was experiencing; and third, he had to be able to come to correctly judge his understanding of these events of his experiment. In his knowing what really was going on, operative in his inquiring was this sublating, dynamic structure of experiencing, understanding, and judging.

Likewise, if knowing demands us to experience, understand and to judge in order to know what knowing itself really is, we have to experience, understand and judge our own 'knowing' process. We shall come to an insight into that experience of our knowing process and then we shall have to judge correctly our understanding of this experience of our experiencing, understanding and judging[15].

How different, then, is 'knowing' from 'being conscious'? Activities that are self-assembling in the knowing process first involve experiencing, or sensing. What does one do when one sees something? What is the activity of understanding, or insight? Let us note that the term 'insight' denotes rather a fresh, new understanding. Lonergan observes that all one has to do is to open and close one's eyes to get to know what seeing is; however, 'insights ... cannot be turned on and off in that fashion'. More attention is

---

15   Cf. B.Lonergan, 2017, p.18, pars.2-4, p.19;

needed to explain and to verify either what understanding is or
what knowing is. To get an insight, firstly one has to be interested
in and be attentive to what could help one catch on to anything.
This requires one to be authentic and really ready to get down
to the elements of a subject and to pay close attention to the
conscious instances of one's own understanding, or failures to
do so. Secondly, one has to observe one's own repeated efforts
to learn something; how, from being genuinely puzzled, one
gets to catch on[16]. Thirdly, as did Inspector Hubbard, one has to
attend to and question the experience of raising and answering
all relevant questions before one can experience, understand
and affirm the existence of a reflective insight. Only with this
experience of a reflective insight does one understand one's
own consciousness of a compulsion that one now can and,
indeed, rationally *has* to proceed to say 'yes' or 'no' to what is
proposed for assent.

Lonergan explains that it is when we are seeing, hearing etc.
that we are experiencing or being conscious of our own sensitivity. And when we are inquiring, understanding, conceiving
and thinking, we are experiencing our own intelligence. Then,
as we are reflecting, weighing the evidence and judging, we are
experiencing our own rationality. Just as rationality differs from
intelligence, which also differs from sensitivity, so in experiencing each of these three, one experiences oneself differently. This
is so because we are conscious of ourselves acting differently
while acting in each of these three different ways.

Again, we can grasp how different consciousness is from
knowing. Knowing knowing is judging our understanding of our
experiencing, understanding and judgement. Consciousness is

---

16   Cf.B.Lonergan, 1988, p.209, par.1

not knowing. Where knowing is always *judging*, being conscious is merely *experiencing*[17].

1.13c Could one carry out an introspection of one's activities?

If Inspector Hubbard were to ask, 'Am I the one arranging this test?' he would not be carrying out 'introspection' in the sense of having a look at himself and a good, long, hard look at his action. One now knows that one does not get to know something merely by taking a good look at it, or by immediately experiencing it, or by merely sensing it. Merely acting on the first level of intentional consciousness is but one element, and the preparatory one, of the compound of conscious, self-assembling activities that is the dynamic of human knowing, nor does one get to know what the object truly is by merely achieving insight into what the object may be, or by attaining to some idea or to some concept of the object. And certainly, one is not in any way knowing something by taking a spiritual, platonic look at some idea of what is understood. To get to know something, one has to be questioning and so not only come to grasp some understanding and express this insight aptly but also reach a reasonable affirmation of this conceived understanding in the data of what one has experienced. Inspector Hubbard showed us this much.

That is, we have to be acting on all *three* levels of intentional consciousness, not just on *one* level, nor even just on *two* levels. Indeed, we have to question what we have understood in the data experienced and then, in addition, we must find if our theory, thereby gained from this theorising, stands up to persistent questioning. The whole three levels have to interact and contribute

---

17   Cf.B.Lonergan , 2017, pp. 11-15, p.102, par.4; Cf.B.Lonergan 1992, pp.344-350; cf. B.Lonergan 1988, pp.208-210

to reaching the reflective insight on the third level of intentional consciousness where we are then in a commanding position to proceed to say 'yes' to what is suggested to be true or real. Then, through rational force of reflective insight and assent, we know for real the possibility that has been suggested as real! Sublation has to have occurred, where the third level in the process of self-transcendence lifts up to a higher level what has been achieved on the prior first and second levels of intentional consciousness.

Can we grasp from our own experience just how different having an insight is from merely looking at something? One needs to experiment with experiences of catching on, of having an insight. We might do this in order to recognize the exact moment an insight occurs for us, then we experience the drive to formulate the characteristics of having an insight correctly[18]. And here, do we experience the drive (intentional notion) arising in us because of our conception to go on to weigh evidence to judge what we have formulated is correct? We are not satisfied for it to be but a possibility; we want to know if it is real. So, we are consciously driven to try to come to a reflective insight verifying what is clearly and distinctly formulated to be correct, just as Chief Inspector so rightly found it imperative to propose his two experiments in regards to finding if the wife knew of the key under the staircase carpet, and finally, if the husband knew[19].

Is looking without understanding therefore just 'gaping'? And just how different is 'conceiving' (formulating the insight) from 'looking'? Remember how the scientist set to work formulating more clearly the unification and organization of the data relevant

---

18   Cf. B.Lonergan 1988, p.208, par.5, p.209.par.1

19   "we conceive in order to judge" B.Lonergan,1992, p.298 par.6. Prof.
      T. Daly nicely defines reality as "that which stands up to persistent
      questioning."

to having the insight that he had experienced in church during the sermon? He needed to put more clearly and to lay more firmly an express hold of the insight he had grasped suddenly and elatedly. A mere look would not have done any such thing.

Just how different is laboriously formulating from just gaping? And further, just how different is 'judging' from 'looking'? It took the Inspector a while to consider data and raise questions before he grasped the insight that Swan could possibly have already replaced the key under the staircase carpet before entering the room, but without all this asking and reasoning and testing, the Inspector could never have grasped this insight. It certainly was not simply a matter of taking a good look that he found this possible lack in Wendice's rearrangement of the data at the crime scene.

We should also note that we do not heighten our being present to ourselves by having a good look inside ourselves. Instead, Lonergan notes, we are more aware of ourselves as we raise the level of our intentional activity! On waking, we become present to ourselves as moving. When faced with a puzzle, we may dispose data promoting our questioning as to how, and indeed we are aware of wondering, asking questions for understanding and are keenly aware of ourselves when suddenly gaining longed-for insight. We then enjoy a greater awareness in being enabled to verify our theory, having longed to do this. So, we are aware of being sensing and intellectual and rational people, and further, we are not happy if we are not acting responsibly[20].

Does such a knowing subject exist? Well, one would surely be slow to say that one did not see or hear, or be intelligently able to have an insight or be rationally able to come to correct

---

20   Cf. B.Lonergan 2017, p.35, par.4

judgement[21]. We noted Inspector Hubbard notice relevant data, obtain insight and reason carefully, and judge and evaluate responsibly. Then, in considering theoretically how we ourselves are knowing subjects, we might also progress from the data of our consciousness to questioning our knowing activities and come to understand them and to judge them[22]. Lonergan invites the reader to do this, not by taking a look inside oneself but by being open to recognising how one in fact likes to be attentive, intelligent, reasonable and responsible and also how one speaks in a way that relies upon one being alert to the questions proper to such self-transcendence. Note too, that on all four levels, 'we are aware of ourselves but, as we mount from level to level, it is a fuller self of which we are aware and the awareness itself is different'[23]. For example, Lonergan points to the saying of de La Rochefoucauld, that everyone might complain of their memory but never of their judgement! 'A judgement is the personal responsibility of the one who judges. It is a personal commitment'.

---

21   Cf. B.Lonergan, 2017, p.20, par.2; also cf.B.Lonergan, 1988, p.210, par.3..

22   Cf.B.Lonergan 1988, pp.208-210; also cf. B.Lonergan 2017, pp.17-22

23   Cf. B. Lonergan, 2017, p.13, par3; p.14.par.1; 1992,297,par.6.

Chapter 2

The cognitional and moral self-transcendence of Chief Inspector Hubbard

2.1 Knowing comprizes experiencing, understanding and judging

From our inquiry so far, we have found that one cannot get to know anything without first noticing things that need to be made sense of and secondly, without succeeding to make sense of the data noticed or to understand it and thirdly, without making sure one has understood it correctly. Through these three successive activities, although these three are quite different, one fully respects the different character of each, and yet one's inquiry is promoted in new dimensions as one carries out each successive, distinctive activity. One proceeds in this integration neither unconsciously nor mechanically, but consciously.

So it was that Inspector Hubbard came to grasp the possibility of the husband having conspired to have his wife murdered. He needed to verify this possibility. Inspector Hubbard needed not only to catch on, via examination of the concrete data, to what Wendice possibly had really conspired to do; he also needed to be the honest man that he was and not be satisfied with mere suspicion and possibility. So, he first needed concrete, pertinent data. Secondly, he needed intelligently to catch on to what Wendice had possibly conspired to do and also set up an appropriate hypothesis. Thirdly, he needed to verify that the idea proposed by the hypothesis was true. Accordingly, driven by his spirit of inquiry, the Inspector had to set up apt experiments that contained final relevant questions in order to grasp final relevant answers. These answers in turn would leave him no further hesitation to give or to refuse his assent to what his hypothesis proposed.

So, we can grasp what Lonergan means by saying that human knowing has many distinct and irreducible activities: first, sensing – seeing, hearing, smelling, touching, tasting, imagining, perceiving; second, inquiring and the properly intellectual activities of understanding, conceiving, formulating and defining; third, these activities of understanding and formulating demand to be followed by further intellectual operations of reflecting, and weighing evidence, in order to grasp reflective insight so that one can judge what is truly the case[24].

Again, Inspector Hubbard first had to act to receive data to question for understanding. Secondly, as he inquired of the data, asking what and why and how, he came up with possible answers. Thirdly, he then reflected and asked further questions, not to gain new possibilities but to verify if these possible answers already proposed were correct. In so doing, by raising all relevant questions, he would gain final answers that would exclude all reasonable doubt. So, after opening the door and turning to make a run for it, Wendice manifested to all in the room that they had arrived at the point of being accurately able to reflect on all relevant questions and had now been rationally compelled to affirm the truth of the case.

---

24   Cf. B. Lonergan, 2017, p.13, par.3; p,14, par.1. Also cf. Lonergan, 2016 (CWL 13) pp.108, par.2, pp.109-110; and Lonergan, 1988(CWL 4), pp.206-208

In summary, Inspector Hubbard carried out three types of activities: attending to pertinent data; questioning this data as to what, how and why, to come to an hypothesis; and finally, to verify what the hypothesis proposed. None of these three types of activities on its own, or none by omitting any of the other two, would have sufficed for Inspector Hubbard to attain knowledge of the truth.

How could the Inspector propose a theory on Swan's death without noting down every bit of pertinent information he could get? He did not just look at the dead body but kept asking why, what and how of the possibly pertinent details. If he did not inquire in order to come to an understanding of the data, he would have been merely 'gaping' at the details presented for his inspection. Certainly he would never have been able to formulate into an hypothesis what he understood from the data.

So, then, just as mere looking at something and seeing is not human knowing, so for the same reason the other sensings – merely hearing, smelling, touching, tasting – may be parts, but only potential components, of human knowing; they are not human knowing itself, yet without sense data, or without the data of one's consciousness, one's memories, experiences etc., one has nothing to understand. Through understanding the data of sensing or of consciousness, one gains – as in the case of Inspector Hubbard – direct insight or understanding of something positive; namely, a possible explanation contained in that presentation of data.

Note, however, that by combining sensing and understanding, these first and second activities together do not get one to know anything. Imagine Chief Inspector Hubbard strolling round the room because he had got an exciting new insight, holding a mere idea of what Wendice had possibly done, and imagine him saying: 'Well, you can all go home now – that's it. That is all we need! We all know now who is guilty after all!' We would be ashamed of him. Actually, we see Halliday, the detective story writer, rushing to judgement, but we can understand him doing this because of his love for Margot, and so perhaps his usual investigative rigour is put aside for the time being.

So it is that getting hold of a bright idea is yet not knowing fact. A just rebuke is handed down to Halliday by none other than Inspector Hubbard who says we have to wait for that apartment door to open and for Wendice to walk in, having used Margot's key, and 'then we will know everything'!

In addition to taking in data and questioning data in order to gain some possible understanding, Inspector Hubbard had to carry out a third type of mind activity. This third mind activity was not to ask further why or how or what or to form a new hypothesis but to ask and determine if the hypothesis he already had proposed was true. He had to find evidence to verify his hypothesis.

The Inspector then proceeded to weigh evidence for or against by asking all the relevant questions. Wendice's opening the door enabled the Inspector to gain the reflective insight that the Inspector's final relevant question was now answered. He now understood he had satisfied the conditions required for him to proceed to say 'yes' to what his hypothesis proposed. Also, once having gained the reflective insight that he had fulfilled all these conditions necessary for him to say 'yes', if he now hesitated to go ahead and give that assent, he would be conscious of being unreasonable. So it was that through his utter conviction evident in his practice (that truth was gained only after gaining the answer to the final relevant question), Chief Inspector Hubbard was able to transcend himself cognitionally, to grasp what was true independent of his own thinking. Lonergan would agree with the integrity of the Inspector's practice as to pronounce judgement without that reflective grasp is merely to guess. Again, what we know is that once that grasp has occurred, then to refuse to judge is just silly[25].

Then again, one does not know simply by judgement alone. One cannot, as Lonergan says above, exclude experiencing and understanding, for if one were to pass judgement on what one did not understand, one would not be knowing anything but simply being arrogant. As well, judging without data prevents one from knowing fact. As Lonergan says: 'To pass judgement independently of all experience is to set fact aside.'[26]

Without Inspector Hubbard's final experiment to find out if Mr Wendice knew of the key under the staircase carpet, he would never have got to know the fact of Wendice's guilt. This demonstrates that human knowing is not just one of these three operations – experiencing, understanding, and judging – nor any combination of two of them apart from the third; but instead, human knowing is the whole of these three operations functioning as a self-assembling, dynamic structure. And this structure is consciously executing its systematic procedure: 'It is self-assembling, self-constituting. It puts itself together, one part summoning forth the next, till the whole is reached. And this occurs, not with the blindness of natural process, but consciously, intelligently, rationally'. Lonergan calls such a structure 'formally dynamic'.[27]

'Experience stimulates inquiry, and inquiry is intelligence bringing itself to act; it leads from experience through imagination to insight, and from insight to the concepts that combine in

25   B. Lonergan, 1992, p.304, par.2

26   B.Lonergan, 1988, 'Cognitional Structure', p.207, par 2

27   B.Lonergan, 1988, 'Cognitional Structure' p.p .207, par.4

single objects both what has been grasped by insight and what in experience or imagination is relevant to the insight. In turn, concepts stimulate reflection and reflection is the conscious exigence of rationality; it marshals the evidence and weighs it either to judge or else to doubt and so renew inquiry'.[28]

2.2   Judging the fact, Inspector Hubbard was conscious of wanting to be responsible

Knowing the fact of Mrs Wendice's innocence, Chief Inspector Hubbard experiences himself driven or wanting to be responsible; that is, he feels he just has to carry out a new duty, indeed a moral duty. He experiences himself driven to be responsible and so to give assent to it being a good thing that Mrs Wendice be set free; then he responsibly decided to ring to inform the Home Secretary.

Note that earlier, the Inspector did not and could not reasonably have proceeded to decide to ring the Home Secretary, for before the husband opened the door, there had not occurred, nor could there have occurred, that final reflective insight in the Inspector's mind. Such an insight could only have occurred by grasping that the final relevant question, if the husband knew of the key being under the staircase carpet, had been answered, and so the conditions had been met, allowing the Inspector to proceed to judgement. By experiencing that reflective insight, he simultaneously experienced in his consciousness the rational force of his mind to bring him to give his assent – yes, the husband is guilty. Inspector Hubbard's hypothesis was now more than a genuine understandable possibility; it was proven to be a verified explanation.

---

28   B.Lonergan, 1988, p.207, par.4

The Inspector was then aware of something new happening in his consciousness: a pressing drive of clear moral responsibility. He now grasped that he had all the reason he needed to proceed and indeed had to proceed responsibly to judge that it was only right and good to act morally to have her set free. It was not that he had to be told. No! He had been brought to understand how significant the final question in his hypothesis was. He was now understanding that the final answer had not only tied together everything in a way that would unify intelligibly and organize all the data of the whole investigation, but more importantly that the answer met the conditions set for assenting to that intelligible unity being a real one. Also, quite consciously, the answer was warranting him to give assent to the fact of her innocence. And not only to give assent to this fact but also now to proceed responsibly to give assent to the value of her innocence.

Now with authority, and with authenticity, he could judge not only the fact of Mrs Wendice's innocence but also that it was only just and right to vindicate Mrs Wendice from her sentence of execution. In this he now felt a responsibility to proceed to act on her behalf. So, we come to note the role of *feelings* in the knowing and deciding process of self-transcendence.

2.3   The role of feelings in transcendental method

Feelings that are non-intentional states or trends: Lonergan says of feelings that they are modes of relating to the world. He begins by distinguishing between affective responses that are intentional and those that are non-intentional.

There are states, conditions or moods such as fatigue, irritability, bad humour, anxiety. These 'feeling-states' have causes. Also, there are trends, urges or drives such as hunger, thirst, sexual discomfort. These 'feeling-trends' have goals. But the state is simply an effect of its cause; the trend is merely to achieve the goal. The relationship is not thought out in any way. 'The feeling does not presuppose and arise out of perceiving, imagining or representing the cause or goal. Rather, one first feels tired and, perhaps belatedly, one discovers that what one needs is a rest, or first one feels hungry and then one diagnoses the trouble as a lack of food.'[29]

I may be in a state of anxiety for the reason or cause that I am failing to finish an assignment on time, or I may be hungry and the goal of this feeling hungry is a good meal.[30] It is not that I first have to imagine or perceive the gravity of not finishing the essay on time, nor do I have to conceive a possibility that I am hungry. Rather, it is that being late with the essay, I then feel anxious at this lateness and I take steps to deal with it, getting the essay done or asking for an extension. Or I happen to begin to feel hungry and as a result, I set about getting something to eat. The feeling occurs and effects a response.

Feelings that are intentional responses now relate us not just to a cause or to a goal; these feelings now relate us to an object that has been perceived, understood, judged to be of value, to be lovable. The feeling is such that it has mass, momentum, drive, power. 'We want this! We feel very strongly about this!' says the dynamic political leader. 'I cannot live without you,' says the lover. Without these types of feelings that are intentional responses, says Lonergan, 'our knowing and deciding would be paper thin', and he gives examples of such feelings.

'Because of our feelings, our desires and our fears, our hope or

---

29   B.Lonergan, 2017, p.31, par 2; p.32, par.1

30   Cf. James B. Sauer, A commentary on Lonergan's method in theology, eds Peter L Monette and Christine Jamieson, The Lonergan web site: www.lonergan.on.ca

despair, our joys and sorrows, our enthusiasm and indignation, our esteem and contempt, our trust and distrust, our love and hatred, our tenderness and wrath, our admiration, veneration, reverence, our dread, horror, terror, we are oriented massively and dynamically in a world mediated by meaning. We have feelings about other persons – we feel for them, we feel with them. We have feelings about our respective situations, about the past, about the future, about evils to be lamented or remedied, about the good that can, might, must be accomplished.'[31]

There is a first type of intentional response. It is to what is perceived as agreeable or disagreeable, satisfying or dissatisfying. One may be disinclined to undergo the labour of working longer hours, but one may need the money; that is, one feels the inconvenience of these longer hours. But it is good that a parent gain the extra income to support one's family. What is disagreeable can then, however, be good.

A second type of intentional response is the feeling for what is of value.[32] A person can very much be of value. A devoted husband keeps a photo of his wife and family on his desk and looks at it and responds with a loving desire to be with them and to give his work and life for them. His loving response is what he feels for them. They are of supreme value to him, and his response to their value for him is his total life's effort. His feeling is for the quality of their lives, the values of their good lives, the personal beauty and the beauty of family life they provide,

---

31   B.Lonergan, 2017, p.32, par.2 We cannot here in this introductory essay treat adequately or summarize Lonergan's work on feelings. Cf. also Andrew Tallon, Head and Heart: affection, cognition, volition as triune consciousness, Fordham University Press, New York, 1997, pp.82-105 passim, additional inquiry into the role of feelings.

32   B.Lonergan, 2017, p.32, par.3, p.33.pars.1, 2..

their understanding and their reciprocal valuing of him as husband and father. He responds to all these values that he knows they have for him. He, in turn, responds to these feelings for the values his family have for him in his total, self-giving love and service and work for them. Such is the mass and momentum of feeling that drives him on in life and why any loss, illness or accident involving his family is catastrophic for him. Sometimes good people in carrying out duties have to do what is disagreeable and undergo privations. [33]

The family man we have been considering is a good husband and good father and wants only what is good for his family. He therefore has to endure the disagreeability of being absent on business trips. At times, too, he has to suffer the unpleasantness of being at odds with his children when they want something that would be harmful for them and he has to refuse them. His feelings about what is good for them outweighs his feelings about being agreeable towards them i.e. his desire for their good outdoes his desire for their agreeable feelings towards him.

2.3a Feelings respond to values in a scale of preference

We may now distinguish vital social, cultural, personal and religious values in an ascending order.

Vital values, such as health and strength, grace and vigour, are normally preferred to avoiding the work, privations and pains involved in acquiring, maintaining, restoring them. Social values, such as the good of order which conditions the vital values of the whole community, have to be preferred to the vital values of individual members of the community.

---

33   B.Lonergan, 2017, p., 32 pars.2, 3 & 4

People will choose to undergo the pain and effort and required privations needed to acquire the vital values, such as health and strength, grace and vigour. For example, an athlete may forgo certain pleasurable foods for competitive excellence, and then it can happen that the consideration of vital values of certain individuals will have to make way for those social values that enable the whole community to keep running as a well-functioning community. For example, the money proposed for a stadium may have to be diverted for the improved services of a police force or a city transit system. Then, such vital and social values are needed to support the pursuit of values found through education and cultural artistic presentations. These cultural interests directly elevate the heart and feelings and mind while the vital and social values indirectly contribute to this elevation, for culture's job is 'to discover, express, validate, criticize, correct, develop and improve such meaning and value' of the way of life people follow. Finally, as a person makes good decisions, and especially loving ones, he inspires others to do so, and true religious values place this loving on a secure basis. [34]

---

34 B.Lonergan, 2017, p.32 par4, p.33, pars.1, 2

Religious values
For central meaning, value of human living.

Personal values
One's self-transcendence
as loving, being loved, originator
of values.

Cultural values
To find,develop, criticize
meaning and value in life above
vital social values.

Social values
for good of order for vital values
of whole community prior to
vital values of individual members of community.

Vital values
for health, grace, vigour prior to
avoiding work, privation.

2.3b   The development of feelings in response to values

One develops one's feelings in order for one to grasp the enormous labyrinth of values one has to respond to during one's life and, in accord with their scale of preferences, one has to be critical while one has to develop one's appropriate intentional responses to these values.

Fundamentally, feelings occur spontaneously. They do not lie under the command of one's decision 'as do the motions of our hands'.[35] Once our feelings have arisen, we may encourage and reinforce them by giving our attention to them and by approving

---

35   B.Lonergan, 2017, p.33.par 2

them, or we may limit them by not giving them our approval and turning our attention away from them. Not only will this approval and curtailment encourage some feelings and discourage others, it will affect our spontaneous scale of preferences. Further, Lonergan adds, as we give praise and discriminatingly pay less heed to this or that object, we can educate others to be discerning as to what is truly meritorious of our feelings of approval and apprehension of values.[36]

Lonergan notes feelings that have been snapped off by repression 'to lead thereafter an unhappy subterranean life'.[37] Feelings such as these can emerge throughout life as jealousy, envy and anger. They lead one to lead a sad and often tragic life of depression and ungenerosity. But then, when fully attended to, noted, understood, expressed and judged of value, and deliberately chosen and encouraged, there are feelings 'so deep and strong, especially when deliberately enforced ... they channel attention, shape one's horizon, direct one's life. Here the supreme illustration is loving'.[38]

Indeed, a man or woman who falls in love is doing so not only attending to the beloved but doing so at all times. Either one can be asked if he or she could attend dinner, say, and the reply will be conditional upon whether they will be both be able to come, for they both carry out their particular acts of loving towards each other and for each other. Also, prior to these acts, they are both in a state of being in love and this state is the fount of all the actions of both partners. So, mutual love is the intertwining of *two* lives, it transforms an 'I' and 'thou' into a 'we' so intimate, so

36   B.Lonergan, 2017 ,p.33. par.2

37   Cf.B. Lonergan, 2017, p.33, par.3

38   B.Lonergan, 2017, p.33.par.3.

secure, so permanent, that each attends, imagines, thinks, plans, feels, speaks, acts in concern for both.[39]

2.3c   The aberration of feeling

Feelings can become distorted and crippled.[40] Lonergan finds the most notable of these is perhaps what has been named 'ressentiment'. It means 'to feel again'. It is not envy, jealousy, or resentment.[41] It is where one experiences again how one felt during a confrontation with another's 'value-qualities'. This 'another' is one's superior in some way either physically, intellectually, morally or spiritually. This re-feeling goes on for a long time, even over a lifetime. At that time, one felt hostile, angry, indignant and never expressed this, or simply put it aside. This re-feeling of hostility attacks the value-quality that the superior person possesses, a value that the inferior not only lacks but also feels unequal to acquiring. And the way the hurt person attacks is to belittle the value in question. Indeed, the re-feeling can give rise to hatred and even to violence against those who possess that value-quality.

But, Lonergan adds, what is worst is that this re-feeling can reject one value to the extent that it distorts a whole scale of values, and 'this distortion can spread through a whole social class, a whole people, a whole epoch'. Much better is it, says Lonergan, to take full cognisance of one's feelings, however deplorable they may be, than to put them aside. To know them and assess them enables one to know oneself, to 'uncover the inattention, obtuseness, silliness, irresponsibility that gave rise

---

39   B.Lonergan, 2017, p.33.par.3;p.34, par.1

40   Saurer, ibid., p.55

41   Saurer, ibid., p.55

to the feeling one does not want, and to correct the aberrant attitude."[42]

If, however, one does not attend to such a feeling, one leaves them conscious but not objectified. Then there can arise a conflict between the self as objectified and the self as conscious. This alienation can lead to misguided remedies and, eventually, it is very necessary that one turn to counselling.[43]

Saurer interprets Lonergan here as meaning that leaving such feelings in the dark and not attended to and objectified entails that feelings can 'direct our choosing without our being aware of it".[44]

2.3d   The sublating role of feelings

Later we shall speak of moral and religious conversions where the key function of feelings will be noticed as intentional responses to values.

Jean Valjean will be so moved in gratitude and shock at the mercy and benevolence of the Bishop towards him that it will cause Jean to constitute a new scale of values to live by, stemming from a new beneficence and benevolence effected by the experience of being loved by the Bishop.

Saint Paul will be so gifted with the shocking experience of unearthly love and goodness towards him that he too would experience and critically set up a new scale of preference of values to live by. He would tell the Philippians that what he had prized most in life he now regarded as but dung in comparison to the values he then prized to live by.

---

42   B.Lonergan, 2017, p.34, par.3

43   Cf. B.Lonergan, 2017, p.34, par.3, p.35.par.1

44   Saurer, ibid., p.56

The feelings Paul expressed were many, and those of one utterly in love with one whom he experienced as one of absolute value. Such can be the effect of being in love upon one's value system.

We now include feelings in our diagram to follow.

2.4   The basic pattern of operations for all knowing: transcendental method

The human spirit is consciously inquiring through four levels of consciousness that bring the human spirit to go beyond itself to its goal to know truly (Level 3) and to decide responsibly what is reasonably morally correct (Level 4).

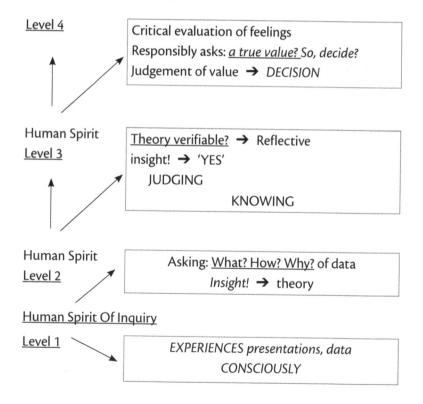

Level 4

Critical evaluation of feelings
Responsibly asks: *a true value? So, decide?*
Judgement of value ➜ *DECISION*

Human Spirit
Level 3

<u>Theory verifiable?</u> ➜ Reflective
insight! ➜ 'YES'
    JUDGING
        KNOWING

Human Spirit
Level 2

Asking: <u>What? How? Why?</u> of data
    Insight! ➜ theory

Human Spirit Of Inquiry

Level 1

EXPERIENCES presentations, data
CONSCIOUSLY

Diagram and revision: We now reflect on this sequence of operations to note that it is a universal one. We question our consciousness as to what, how and why in order that we get a fresh understanding or insight. We begin to find the words that fit exactly what we intelligently have caught hold of. We might form a theory. We then no longer want another theory, for the moment. Our attention is taken up with our present theory; we just have to question if it could be true.

To do this, we ask all the relevant questions needed to test our theory. We have to reason for and against. We might be able to get to the point where we grasp that we have found the final relevant question, and on achieving an answer, we are aware we need go no further in our questioning, for we would be silly to ignore the sufficient evidence we have. We feel rationally compelled to give our assent, for we have met the conditions required by the hypothesis to be able to give our assent to its being verified. This assent gives birth within us to an awareness of having to be responsible and to do the thing we now know to be the reasonable and moral and right thing to do. We act this way. So, we may name what we seek on the four various levels, the transcendentals namely, the experiential data, the intelligible, the true, the good.

2.5 Diagram: human intentionality

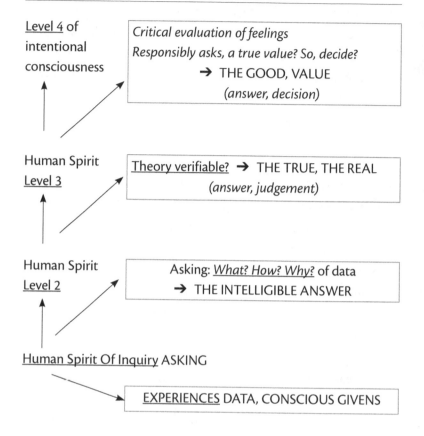

Level 4 of intentional consciousness

> *Critical evaluation of feelings*
> *Responsibly asks, a true value? So, decide?*
> → THE GOOD, VALUE
> *(answer, decision)*

Human Spirit Level 3

> Theory verifiable? → THE TRUE, THE REAL
> *(answer, judgement)*

Human Spirit Level 2

> Asking: *What? How? Why?* of data
> → THE INTELLIGIBLE ANSWER

Human Spirit Of Inquiry ASKING

> EXPERIENCES DATA, CONSCIOUS GIVENS

The one human spirit inquires and puts many questions in pursuit of a single goal. This human spirit of inquiry raises universal questions for intelligence, for judging, and for deliberating, and too it unites them. These universal questions are: 'What is this? How is this so? Why is this so?' and then we raise the questions: 'Is this so? Is this true?' of what we have found to be a possibility. Only then can we ask: 'Is what is true here of real value that can be honoured and acted upon?' Our questions in this order have enabled us to go beyond ourselves to what is so, to what is true i.e. Mrs Wendice's innocence.

On the side of the object being questioned are won, accumulatively, partial elements gained in corresponding answers to the questions. These answers to such are concrete realizations of the transcendentals – namely, those elements intended in the above universal questions. These answers denote elements ascertained in ascending order – the intelligible and the possible, the true, the real and the good – and these answers that are realized in that order thereby form into a single whole.

Again, this unity and whole is the object under question: is Mrs Wendice innocent? Questioning then proceeds in order. Mrs Wendice, now presented as possibly being innocent can be verified as being really and truly innocent. Accordingly, she must proceed to being judged as innocent, and with her being judged as truly innocent, she has to have the Home Secretary respect this value of being innocent and carry out the decision in favour of her being released. A vindicated and free Mrs Wendice is the unity ascertained by this ordered questioning process.

And this unity and whole that is known and decided for is the justified and liberated Mrs Wendice: her liberation is achieved by the Inspector's self-transcending activities to get beyond himself, the knowing subject, to what is independently intelligible, true, real and good. This good has been achieved by a method that engenders self-transcendence, cognitional and moral.

Inspector Hubbard proceeded successfully to find out who in fact was guilty of the killing of Mr Swan. In fact his procedure, we can notice, was to take in relevant information, inquiring all along; firstly, as to why was Swan killed; secondly, forming a possible theory; thirdly, seeking to verify it by re-examining it and, in response to final relevant questioning, forming a new hypothesis that he proved correct. Fourthly, he then responsibly rang the Home Secretary to report of his finding that would in fact be valuable as being the necessary condition for setting Mrs Wendice free from a false conviction. All very natural procedure for a thoroughly inquiring, intelligent, reasonable and responsible person.

So, Inspector Hubbard's many activities or operations, experiences, understanding, judgements and decisions link together in that the intelligible oneness grasped by insight is verified in judgement as being truly so independent of his mind, and so real. Also, then the real value of Mrs Wendice's innocence is affirmed and decided upon and acted upon by Inspector Hubbard's ringing the Home Secretary. Thus the many questions proper to each level of conscious intending conspire in order to know what is intelligible, true and good, for the Inspector was inquiring intelligently to understand by asking what, how and why of the data being presented. Next he was reasoning, weighing arguments for and against judging if what is understood and conceived or formulated was true and so real. Then he was responsibly inquiring further to deliberate if what he judged as fact was of true value and so to be decided upon and chosen. His questioning proceeding from his inquiring spirit united all these inquiries and their answers.

On the side of the subject, the Inspector's mind, the one mind, puts many questions in order to gain his goal, the correct decision of liberating Mrs. Wendice. All the answers are parts that gradually accumulate and conjoin into a single whole. Intelligibilities grasped by successive insights into sense data. Conceptions grasping both what sensings perceived and intelligence grasped. Judging what was true in the conceiving and real in what was conceived. Decisions that upheld the values of possibilities affirmed. Also, we find that the transcendentals, namely, the intelligible, the true, the real, and the good apply to absolutely every object in that they come from the successive stages in our dealing with objects. We find too, that they are a unity in their very source, the intending subject. For Inspector Hubbard intended first of all the good, but to achieve it he had to know what was real. But to know what was real he had to know truly what was so. And to know this he had to catch on to what was intelligible and possible, and to grasp what was intelligible he had to attend to the data of sense and of consciousness.[45]

---

45 Human knowing, is a dynamic structure 'a whole whose parts are operations....a structure...one part summoning forth the next, till the whole is reached....consciously, , intelligently, rationally. Experience stimulates inquiry, and inquiry is intelligence bringing itself to act; it leads from experience through imagination to insight, and from insight to the concepts... (which) in turn stimulate reflection, ...(which is)the conscious exigence of rationality; it marshals the evidence and weighs it either to judge or else to doubt and so renew inquiry.' B.Lonergan, 1998' Cognitional Structure' p.207.pars.2-4.

2.6 Diagram: seeking the transcendentals in the self-assembling structure of knowing and deciding

Level 4

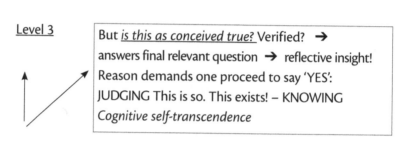

Critical evaluation of feelings
Responsible subject asks: _What is true value?_
Shall I decide in accord with this true value
Judgement of value ➜ _Decision_
Moral self-transcendence

Level 3

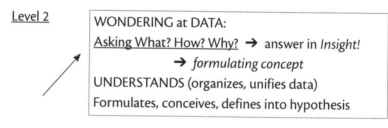

But _is this as conceived true?_ Verified? ➜
answers final relevant question ➜ reflective insight!
Reason demands one proceed to say 'YES':
JUDGING This is so. This exists! – KNOWING
Cognitive self-transcendence

Level 2

WONDERING at DATA:
Asking What? How? Why? ➜ answer in _Insight!_
➜ _formulating concept_
UNDERSTANDS (organizes, unifies data)
Formulates, conceives, defines into hypothesis

Spirit Of Inquiry

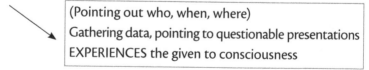

(Pointing out who, when, where)
Gathering data, pointing to questionable presentations
EXPERIENCES the given to consciousness

We also note that we usually do such distinct activities (see diagram above) – sensing, seeing, hearing etc., inquiring, imagining, understanding, conceiving, formulating, reflecting, marshalling and weighing the evidence, judging, deliberating, evaluating, deciding, speaking, doing, writing – while fully aware of ourselves doing these actions, yet we do not know we are doing them, inasmuch as we are focusing upon and directing our inquiry onto the results of these actions rather than onto the actions themselves.

2.7 Transcendental notions are the dynamism of our conscious intentionality

The human spirit is consciously inquiring through levels of consciousness 1 to 4. It is intending self-transcendence in knowing (level 3) and in deciding (level 4).

Inspector Hubbard had been inquiring or intending to know what made sense and what really was the case; he had experienced an interest or drive to understand (transcendental notion aiming at understanding) that was satisfied when understanding was reached in an intelligible, satisfactory hypothesis. Then he experienced a drive to know if his hypothesis was true (transcendental notion driving him to get to know the truth).

His experience in his being driven to truth compelled his assent when he had reached sufficient reason in his reflective insight. Only then was he conscious of a particular responsibility, of a drive to value that brought him to assent to the good of Mrs Wendice being vindicated, and to decide in accord with that affirmed good to act for that good.

Accordingly, upon Wendice walking through the door, and the reflective insight that Wendice occasioned in the Inspector and in all standing inside the room, the Inspector was aware of a drive to be responsible and so to inform the Home Secretary of Mrs Wendice's innocence to get her set free. His success was rewarded with a happy conscience. In this cognitive and moral self-transcendence (his reaching knowing fact and his choosing a value that did exist beyond himself and independent of his own activity), the Inspector achieved the goal of the intending of his conscious intentionality.

Intending the goal is not *knowing* it. We intend the goal in virtue of our transcendental notions, for 'the transcendental notions are the fount not only of initial questions but also of further questions'. These are drives we are conscious of, whereby we seek what is intelligible, true, real and good or of value. The transcendental notions are not abstract; they intend all that one knows and all that remains to be known. They are comprehensive, they intend everything about everything. By them we intend the concrete; namely, all that is to be known about a thing.[46]

Inspector Hubbard would not cease his critical questioning and weighing of evidence until he had raised and answered the final relevant question, then he knew the real and the concrete; he had no questions left to be dealt with. The transcendental notions are the set of natural drives towards knowing the concrete and towards responsibly choosing the concrete. The dynamism of human conscious intentionality is content only with what is critically affirmed as true, real and of value and responsibly and critically chosen and carried out. Questions keep arising for fuller understanding and

---

46   The transcendental notions are "utterly concrete". And "the concrete is the real not under this or that aspect but under its every aspect in its every instance." Lonergan, 2017, p.36, par.3 "But the transcendental notions are not only the fount of initial questions but also of further questions" for "fuller understanding, …and fuller truth".ibid.2017, p.36, par.3. The transcendental notions are not a matter of knowing but of intending. Lonergan , 2017. p.35, par.2; The "transcendental notions are the dynamism of conscious intentionality. They promote the subject from lower to higher levels of consciousness, …." Ibid.p.35, par.3.

fuller explanation, and further doubts urging to a fuller truth. This ever fuller understanding and explanation is achieved by the transcendental notions calling for and structuring a fuller whole that is being achieved by experiencing, understanding and judging – to know fact. So one then is in a position to make decisions and thereby change the world for good. So, one has to ask what is of value, to decide responsibly on the fourth level of intentional consciousness. Again, transcendental method, as conceived by Lonergan, is 'the concrete and dynamic unfolding of human attentiveness, intelligence, reasonableness and responsibility'.[47]

---

47   B.Lonergan, 2017, p.26, par 2; "Again, transcendental method is coincident with a notable part of what has been considered philosophy, but it is not any philosophy or all philosophy. Very precisely, it is a heightening of consciousness that brings to light our conscious and intentional operations and thereby leads to the answers to three basic questions. What am I doing when I am knowing? Why is doing that knowing? What do I know when I do it? The first answer is a cognitional theory. The second is an epistemology. The third is a metaphysics, where however, the metaphysics is transcendental, an integration of heuristic structures, and not some categorial speculation that reveals that all is water, or matter, or spirit, or process, or what have you." Ibid., 2017, p.27, par, 1.

2.8 Intentional notions drive one consciously through the four level questions

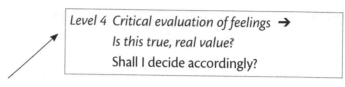

Level 4 *Critical evaluation of feelings* →
Is this true, real value?
Shall I decide accordingly?

Human Spirit
Aiming at, driving on further through fourth level questions

Level 3
Is the concept put forward true?

Human Spirit
Aiming at, driving on further through third level questions

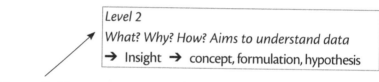

Level 2
What? Why? How? Aims to understand data
→ Insight → concept, formulation, hypothesis

Human Spirit
Aiming at, driving on further through second level questions

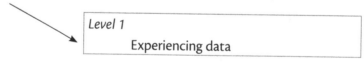

Level 1
Experiencing data

Transcendental notions are drives we are conscious of; firstly, to be intelligent and seek to get to know what is understandable or intelligible; secondly, the drive to be rational brings us consciously to seek to get to know what is in fact true; and thirdly, the intentional notion to be responsible drives us to know and to decide in accord with what we judge to be of correct value. Such is our desire to know and to decide through means of asking questions for each level of conscious intentionality.

We note, importantly, that each set of questions answered ushers in the next set spontaneously. Each new set proper to be asked lifts us up into a new level of conscious intentionality. Note the proper sets of questions belonging to each of the four levels of consciousness (see diagram above) aiming at or tending toward those goals.[48]

The transcendental notions are radical intentions that move us from ignorance to knowledge. They are *apriori* in that they get us beyond what we know to seek what we do not yet know. They are unrestricted in that answers give rise to further questions, comprehensive in that they intend the unknown whole or totality. This totality of answers yet reveals only a fraction of intelligence and gets us answers as to what, why and how. Reason then questions these answers as to whether they are true or not.

Responsibility then goes on to what is really good. If we objectify the contents of these intentions, we have transcendental concepts of the intelligible, the true, the real, the truly good and what is of value, but these are not the transcendental notions that operate to achieving the results that are these conceived contents.[49]

---

48   B.Lonergan, 2017,p.35,pars.3&4; p.36; p.315.par.2

49   Cf. B. Lonergan, 2017,p.15.par.2.

Lonergan notes that it would be a mistake to infer that the transcendental notions are abstract: 'on the contrary they are utterly concrete, for the concrete is the real, not under this or that aspect but under its every aspect in its every instance.' The transcendental notions not only initiate but carry through questions that belong to the four levels of conscious intentionality.[50]

2.9   Sublating

We have said that each set of questions of the four levels of intentionality properly attains the results of each for the next set of questions. One is first conscious of experiencing data being presented and being noticed and being pointed to as to who and when and where and being assembled for questioning for intelligence. Intelligence immediately levels questions on this assembled data asking what, why and how. Eventually one will arrive at a fourth level, where one is raising questions on value and decision. That which each lower level has achieved, the next level of diverse questioning takes over and organizes into a higher unity and purpose. It is called 'sublating'.

For example, we undertake the second-level labour of asking what, why, how, to gain direct insight (direct in finding an intelligibility within the data being examined) into a possibility that is being presented in data on one's first-level experience. Here on this second level of understanding, our insight directly finds for us some unity and organization in the data, or some idea as to how things fit together.

---

50   B.Lonergan, 2017,p.15, par.2.

2.9a Sublating within the four levels of conscious intentionality

We express the intelligibility that the insight contains into a concept. This labour of conception and formulation wins for us a clear and distinct idea of what the insight achieved for us.

Insight grasps neither a given datum of sense nor some imagination but 'an intelligible organization that may or may not be relevant to the data'. Conceiving intends to put together the content of the insight and that much of the image as is required for the insight to occur.[51]

So, we need this idea that insight gains for us to be clearly expressed in a concept or theory. Else we will lose it. Then, our third-level seeking or intending the truth now asks: is the idea that is clearly conceived and expressed true and verifiable?

The idea has to be tested in concrete data. Inspector Hubbard had Mrs Wendice use the key that was in her purse to try to open her door. He was testing to find if she really did not know her key was missing from her purse and if she did know of its being under the staircase carpet outside the door. The Inspector's hypothesis was then that if the key was still there, and if Mr Wendice could provide evidence that he knew it was there in its hiding place, then they had their answer i.e. Wendice had indeed conspired with Swan to murder Mrs Wendice. Of course, the hypothesis had to be verified. A test had to be carried out. One conceives theories, but these have to be tested in the concrete situation where final, relevant questioning reaches an invulnerable insight that clearly stands up to persistent questioning.[52]

---

51 Cf. B.Lonergan, 2017, p.14, par.2

52 'How is concrete actual existence known? Is it through inspection or intuition? Or is it through true judgment? "Truth formally is found

Lonergan asks is the concrete universe, the universe of being known by true judgment. He goes on to say,' I should say that it is. To know the concrete in its concreteness is to know all there is to be known about each thing. To know all there is to be known about each thing is, precisely, to know being. For me, then, 'being' and 'the concrete' are identical terms'.[53]

The second level of intentionality questions of why, how and what? sought understanding of the data presented and sought for what could be made into a possible explanation i.e. what does this data mean? What idea can one get from seeing the dead man lying there? Then more data began to surface and become questioned. The Inspector wondered why Mrs Wendice had lied to him. He did not know she had been carrying out her husband's malevolent instruction to do so. This prevarication on her part, together with the clues left by the husband as hints pointing at possible guilty behaviour on her part, disposed data for the Inspector to obtain an insight unifying the restricted amount

---

only in judgment; and existence is the act of being". "only possible answer is that prior to the act of judgment there occurs a grasp of the unconditioned. For only the unconditioned can ground the objectivity of truth, its absolute character , its independence of the viewpoints, attitudes, orientation of the judging subject." B.Lonergan, 1988, p.150, par.2, 3. Only God has no conditions whatever, is formally unconditioned; but in reflective understanding we grasp what are the conditions of an unconditioned and that these are fulfilled. Then we experience the drive to be rational and pass judgment correctly.Cf. 1988.p.150.par.4; also, again, when "The conditions of the conditioned may be fulfilled, then the conditioned is virtually an unconditioned; it has the properties of an unconditioned, not absolutely, but de facto."1988, p.213, par.2

53   B.Lonergan, 1988, "Insight: Preface to a discussion", p. 148, par. 2

of data that he had been given. The Inspector did then grasp an idea that Mrs Wendice could possibly have planned to do away with her blackmailer. This idea that the Inspector came to grasp seemed to shock him, so it was with some solemnity that he had to warn her that when she went to the station, this time she tell only the truth!

At the station, questions were pursued more intensely as they checked on her story and questioned too her own new evidence that conflicted with evidence given by the husband which did not support her version of things. Her affair with Halliday was brought out. It strongly began to appear that she was being black-mailed by Swan over her affair with Halliday. All these factors began to point to the possible theory of her doing away with Swan.

The jury raised the third level of intentionality questioning; namely, was this theory verifiable? They came to judge this theory as *more* than possible; they found this to be fact. Her affair with Halliday, as Wendice reminded Halliday, lost her the sympathy of the jury. But now, after the trial, the Inspector had gained a new insight from the new relevant data coming in from the behaviour of Mr Wendice. The Inspector raised questions pertaining to the second level of intentional consciousness (why, what and how?). He gained new insight and conceived a conse-quent new hypothesis in which the husband was being proposed as the guilty one.

Then arose the question: is this true? Finally, if proof was forthcoming on the third level of intentional questioning and verification, and the fact of the husband being the guilty party were established, there would then arise the fourth-level inten-tional questions as to the value of Mrs Wendice's innocence being confirmed and her being exonerated and set free. That is, the Inspector would become aware he was consciously driven to carry out a fourth type of questioning; namely, would not the now proven fact of Mrs Wendice's innocence be of true and real value? And accordingly, should he not be responsible and decide to act in accord with this new value rationally affirmed and promote her newly found merited liberation as he would be in duty bound?

Each type of questioning – namely; for understanding, judging, and deciding – proceeded in sequential order, each consciously calling forth the next set of questions. This drive to be responsible and to act rationally and morally could only draw upon the true fact affirmed by the experience, understanding and judgement of Inspector Hubbard. His judgement of fact stimulated in his consciousness the drive to know her innocence as value and to enact respect for that value by his deciding and correspondingly acting to get her set free.

Clearly, then, it is evident that the drive to be responsible, that seeks to judge value and to decide accordingly, built upon and drew all the prior intentionality of the Inspector's cognitional self-transcendence to a higher point of achieved unity. What was intelligible, true and real was now also correctly valued and rationally decided upon and responsibly acted upon. The Inspector's moral self-transcendence now sublated his cognitional self-transcendence.

2.9b Diagram: sublating

DECIDING sublates judging

Sublating ---------

Sublating
Preserves with new operation,
puts on new basis, brings to
fuller realization, sets up higher
principle for extending range of lower level

JUDGING sublates understanding

Sublating ---------

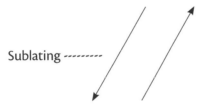

UNDERSTANDING sublates experiencing

Sublating ---------

EXPERIENCING

Lonergan refers to the unity obtained within the levels of intentionality, a unity effected by the sublating of the lower levels by the higher levels. For Different levels of consciousness succeed each other. In such succeeding levels different operations construct objects into larger wholes, in such a way that the one same spirit of inquiry conjoins the products of these different levels of conscious activity into a single compound that is knowing. These succeeding stages result from the 'unfolding of a single thrust, the eros of the human spirit'. For to know the good, Lonergan continues, one has to let unfold one's spirit of inquiry in order to come to know what is real, but in order to get to what is real, one has had to be able to affirm what is true. But for this to happen one has had to get to formulation and verification of hypotheses assembled because of insight into relevant data.[54] Also, Lonergan adds, the conscious subject in coming to a decision can discern value proper to what his intelligence and judgment have grasped as various possible and real options. [55]

Again, Lonergan stresses 'the level of deliberation, evaluation, decision, action – sublates the prior levels of experiencing, understanding, judging. It goes beyond them, sets up a new principle and type of operations, directs them to a new goal but, so far from dwarfing them, preserves them and brings them to a far fuller fruition ...[56]

54   B.Lonergan, 2017, p.16, par.3 .

55   B.Lonergan, 2017,p.16,par.3

56   B.Lonergan 2017, p.294 par.4 "sublation"

2.9c Sublation, enacted by the transcendental notions that proceed under the pure desire to know, promotes the triple cord of objectivity

Intending or wondering aims at that which is, but it merely aims at it; however, the actual activities of insights, hypotheses, tests, reflective insights and answers all conspire to reach the truth – the higher activities sublating and making use of the lower ones to reach this goal of knowing what is real. All the activities required for knowing all build up or contribute under promotion by the pure desire to know, to end with the whole truth.

Without the insight that the husband had been acting suspiciously, the hypothesis of his guilt would not have come about. Without the experiments thought out by the Inspector, the final relevant questions could neither have been formulated nor proposed nor answered. And without the answer to the final relevant question of whether Wendice knew the whereabouts of his wife's missing key, the Inspector could not have gained the reflective insight that demanded his giving assent to the husband's guilt. And without that conscious emanation, he could not have rationally given assent.

So, the transcendental notions, the drives to understand the data, to judge the concepts, in their sublating levels of intending, yield partial objects. These partial cognitional objects (the insight into data, the concepts, the hypothesis, the correct judgement of hypothesis, the affirmed truth) will structure the whole content known that is aimed at by the pure desire to know. It is then that a compound of these activities – experiencing, understanding and judgement – make up actual objectivity where no mere one of these activities suffices! It is all these structured activities working together that attains true knowing of the object. The pure desire to know, the intentionality of human cognitional activity, enables one to be objective at all stages.[57]

So one first has to be objective in attending to all relevant data, experientially objective. Secondly, one has to dispose this data till insight is gained to enable one to figure out adequate formulation and hypotheses. Then one seeks to verify and to test one's hypothesis. By so being intelligent and rational one is then being normatively objective. By raising and by answering all relevant questions one succeeds in gaining the final relevant answer, in which one has to proceed to give assent to something real and now unconditioned, for conditions have been met to do so. This reflective insight and assent is having absolute objectivity.[58]

It was the experiential element needed for Inspector Hubbard's hypothesis to be proven that was presented as Wendice opened the door with his wife's key. This event disposed the data for the final relevant question to be answered and for the Inspector to grasp in reflective insight that he did have his man. This reflective insight of Inspector Hubbard enabled the Inspector to grasp he had met the conditions for proceeding to give assent to the husband's guilt.

So, we have three stages or elements in the objectification process: first, the data or experiential element; second, the normative element of the understanding and hypothesis and weighing of evidence; and third, the absolute element in the reflective insight grasping that the hypothesis has its conditions fulfilled.[59]

---

57   B.Lonergan, 1988, p.213, pars.2&3

58   B Lonergan, 1988, Cognitional structure, p. 213, par 1.

59   B.Lonergan, Ibid. pp.213, 214..

Chapter 3

Objectivity, cognitional self-transcendence and the critical problem

Diagram: The spirit of inquiry and its drives to act experientially, intelligently, reasonably, responsibly by carrying out relevant notional questions in sublation

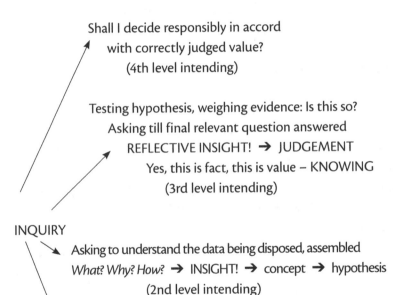

Shall I decide responsibly in accord
with correctly judged value?
(4th level intending)

Testing hypothesis, weighing evidence: Is this so?
Asking till final relevant question answered
REFLECTIVE INSIGHT! → JUDGEMENT
Yes, this is fact, this is value – KNOWING
(3rd level intending)

INQUIRY

Asking to understand the data being disposed, assembled
What? Why? How? → INSIGHT! → concept → hypothesis
(2nd level intending)

Experiencing data being assembled by intelligent inquiry pointing
for inquiry as to who, when, where?
(1st level of intending)

3.1 Objectivity

3.1a Normative objectivity

Insofar as one is intelligently seeking insight in data and weighing evidence in order to be able to verify some proposition, one is carrying out objectivity that is normative.

It took Augustine years, Lonergan notes, to get the insight that something did not have to be bodily and empirical in order to be real.[60] Yet Augustine was writing superbly in commonsense mode and was acting as one intellectually converted, but at that time there was not yet evolved the theoretical explanation of cognitive interiority; namely, the theory of knowing, objectivity and reality according to the intentional notions, the levels of conscious intentionality etc. for him to be able to be guided by an account of intellectual conversion in the theoretical mode.

Those who are intellectually converted, through heightened consciousness have inquired into their inquiry and knowing and have grasped and verified that the real is not just the sense-given, nor just the understood, but is that which is verified. Did Inspector Hubbard not in some way act towards this principle when he said that neither he nor Mr Halliday could say Mrs Wendice was really innocent until he had asked and answered those penultimate and ultimate questions; namely, did Mrs Wendice know of the key hidden under the carpet and, finally, did Mr Wendice know the key was there? Only then, as the Inspector claimed, would he be able to verify that innocence, because for him, in actual practice the real was the verified, though he had not philosophized about it in clear, defined theoretical terms. He was not formally converted intellectually, not having spelt out his position on knowing and sharply defined it against naïve realism.[61]

---

60   Cf. B.Lonergan, 1992, p.15, par.2

61   Cf. B.Lonergan, 2017, p.223, par.4, p.224, par.2; Also, "There are then,

Lonergan says: 'Our own position contained in the canon of parsimony was that the real is the verified; it is what is to be known by the knowing constituted by experience and inquiry, insight and hypothesis, reflection and verification'.[62]

Inspector Hubbard intended to be objective in his investigation. He would not suffer the least obscurantist hiding of truth, so he placed no restriction on data pertinent to his inquiry. Also, he could not permit any human feeling or any favouritism to sway him from conducting his investigation with complete thoroughness, as he was detached from any interfering human inhibition being placed in his way. He would not allow any other curiosity or desire to distract him from the purpose of his inquiry and from the admission of all pertinent data.[63] In fact, Inspector Hubbard was being objective as he was relying upon the untrammelled operation of, as Lonergan names this,

---

two quite disparate meanings of the term 'object'. There is the 'object' in the world mediated by meaning…" and there is also 'object' in the "world of immediacy" . Cf. Lonergan, 2017, p.246, pars.3-4; p.247, par.2; and points out that.."an authentic subjectivity" is gained as one, as critical realist, removes the "ambiguities underlying naïve realism, naïve idealism, empiricism, critical, idealism, absolute idealism…"p.248, par.3

62   B.Lonergan, 1992, 277, par, 3.

63   Normative objectivity opposes 'the subjectivity of wishful thinking, of rash or excessively cautious judgments, of allowing joy or sadness, hope or fear, love or detestation to interfere with the proper march of cognitional process' cf. B.Lonergan, 1992, p.404, par.3; the ' naïve realist knows the world mediated by meaning, but he fancies that he knows it by taking a good look at what is going on out there now.' 2017, P.247.par.2.On individual and group and general biases. Cf.B.Lonergan, 1992, pp244-263.

the 'pure, unrestricted, detached, disinterested desire to know', for normative objectivity is based upon:

> ... the unfolding of the unrestricted, detached, disinterested desire to know. Because it is unrestricted, it opposes the obscurantism that hides truth or blocks access to it in whole or in part. Because it is detached, it is opposed to the inhibitions of cognitional process that arise from other human desires and drives. Because it is disinterested, it is opposed to the well-meaning but disastrous reinforcement that other desires lend cognitional process only to twist its orientation into the narrow confines of their limited range.[64]

What forms normative objectivity, Lonergan continues, is the inner demanding of the pure desire without restriction seeking its goal. The pure desire to know, by desiring to understand and by desiring to come to reflective insight, aims for the universe of being. So, in this way one is being correctly and normatively objective inasmuch as one allows no bias or hindrance to prevent the pure desire from totally free exercise in its questions for understanding and for reflection. Also, the pure desire or the spirit of inquiry can distinguish between questions that allow for answers that solve problems, and other questions, though similar, that presently do not admit solutions. The pure desire can distinguish meaningful questions from those that lack coherence, for the pure desire not only desires; it desires intelligently and reasonably; 'it desires to understand because it is intelligent, and it desires to grasp the unconditioned because it desires to be reasonable.'[65]

Our desire to know aims at the universe of being.

---

64   B.Lonerga1992, p.404, par.4

65   B.Lonergan, 1992,p.404, par.5; and p.405,par.1.

Firstly, our knowledge of the real is not knowledge of some
note or aspect or quality of things; the whole of each thing is
real, and by reality we mean nothing less than the universe in
the multiplicity of its members, in the totality and individuality of each, in the interrelations of all. To know the real is
to know the universe. As our intellects are potential, so our
knowledge of the real is a development.[66]

As we grow in knowledge from our youth onwards, our
knowledge develops by being 'discriminating, differentiating,
categorising' in a scheme we had all along since becoming intelligent. To say something is real, we simply assign it a place in
the universal scheme abovementioned out of which we operate. And that scheme is that all that *is* can be questioned for
understanding and for judgement. All, then, is intelligible. This
scheme itself is that we actuate our capacity to conceive something 'and rationally affirm its existence and its relations'.

> To say that any 'X' is real is just to assign it a place in that
> scheme; to deny the reality of any 'Y' is to deny it a place in the
> universal scheme ... And in its details the scheme is just the
> actuation of our capacity to conceive any essence and ratio-
> nally affirm its existence and its relations.[67]

Inspector Hubbard allowed free rein to his pure desire to know,
his spirit of inquiry, and he did so intelligently and reasonably.
He followed his spirit of inquiry, the demand for intelligibility
and the demand for the unconditioned. He thereby fulfilled
the requirements of normative objectivity. He did not deal

---

66   B.Lonergan, 1997, p.98, par.2
67   B.Lonergan, 1997, p.98, pars.2, 3

with pertinent data as something merely to be looked at – no! Rather, any such given data in the Wendices' apartment was for him to be questioned for understanding to be found, and this understanding had to be formulated in an hypothesis which was to be questioned by reasonable weighing of evidence. By this weighing of evidence, he could move rationally from what was possible to the grasping of sufficient evidence. Such was normative objectivity that promoted him now to be able and ready to grasp in a reflective insight that evidence was now sufficient.

He could now attain absolute objectivity by actually understanding in reflection that he had answered all the relevant questions fulfilling the conditions for him to give assent to that possibility proposed by hypothesis to be true and real. So, then, in point of fact, he was attaining to what was real, not by naïvely looking at something given to be looked at or blindly without reason affirming it. Instead, his practice manifested that something was immediately real for him only in this, that he could rigorously question it. We could say that insofar as anything could be a goal for his unrestricted desire to know, it first was given as data for questioning for his understanding and judgement. Of this desire to know, Lonergan says:

> ... to be objective, in the normative sense of the term, is to give free rein to the pure desire, to its questions for intelligence, and to its questions for reflection ... Because all objectivity rests upon the unrestricted, detached, disinterested desire to know. It is that desire that sets up the canons of normative objectivity. It is that desire that gives rise to the absolute objectivity implicit in judgement.[68]

---

68   B.Lonergan, 1992, p.404, par.5; also p.407,par.4. "all objectivity rests

3.1b Experiential objectivity

The experiential part of objectivity, Lonergan explains, is 'the given (data)'. The given is made up of material one asks about and in which one finds conditions to be fulfilled to verify the theory to arrive at the unconditioned.

Before he began his criminal inquiry, the Inspector had made no selection of people of interest for police investigation. Before inquiry, Lonergan says, there can be no intelligent discrimination and no reasonable rejection, but when Inspector Hubbard first rang the doorbell of the Wendices' apartment, he did so with one purpose: he wanted to carry out inquiry as to who had broken the law. For this he had to intelligently select for notice data as to who was killed and when the person was killed and where exactly this occurred. He happened to notice other persons, but he was gathering only pertinent data. He recorded only these findings and those histories of others that could be of interest for his inquiry. That is, the Inspector had to be intelligent in his selection of data being presented for notice, for he wanted only what was pertinent to his inquiry and had to leave unselected data behind as a residue.

The given left behind as residue contained differences, but as long as these were not indicated or assigned, they remained only that; namely given, irrelevant data. The identities of other policemen present in the room remained unselected for attention and inquiry. They were part of the empirical residue.

So it is that with inquiry comes screening of data. Also, Lonergan continues, we use 'given' in the broad sense to include not only the sense presentations but also images, dreams, illusions,

---

upon the unrestricted, detached, disinterested desire to know... p.407, par.4; Cf. Lonergan, 1997, pp.98-99.

subjective bias, etc. In order for Inspector Hubbard to be able to inquire into the death of a Mr Swan, he had to collect data from the scene of the killing and eventually later in his reflections on data and theories achieved, he had to set tests to prove his theories. So, to actually come to know if what he might propose as true depended on the data given for the setting up of inquiries and reflections, and these eventually originated the nests of judgements.

So, we understand given as not only what the natural sciences inquire into but also as materials for inquiry by psychologists, cultural historians and others.[69]

But data as data are indubitable. That Swan was dead could not be denied. What can be doubted is an idea or theory on whether or not Mr Wendice knew of the key under the carpet. Actual knowing could only come after a question for reflection put by way of test, and it would be either yes or no. But the given – data – are not an answer to any question, for the given is prior to questioning and independent of any answers. The given is indubitable. The given can also be residual, such as the policemen present at the crime scene, who remained unquestioned. Such given of itself is diffuse and just present, not in any order.

The data he collected were proper to the Inspector's spirit of inquiry, his desire to know about this killing, and these data that were allowed facilitated questioning for gaining insight that

---

69 Lonergan uses the term given in a broad sense. The term given "simply notes that reflection and judgment presuppose understanding, that inquiry and understanding presuppose materials for inquiry and something to be understood. Such presupposed materials will be unquestionable and indubitable, for they are not constituted by answering questions." Cf. B.Lonergan, 1992, p.406, par 7; p.407, pars.1-2

would allow him to formulate an hypothesis. And so proceeded normative objectivity.

The Inspector persisted with his intelligent questioning, accumulating insights, and through his rational questioning weighed up reasons for and against in order to find answers to final relevant questions; namely, did Mrs Wendice know of the key being under the carpet on the staircase outside the apartment and then did Mr Wendice know of the existence of this key?

One notes here that the level of understanding is quite distinct from the level of reasoning for judgement. Inquiring into the nature of things belongs to second-level activity. Inquiring then on the third level of intending, if things are really as one thinks them to be, is a reflection upon what is understood on the second level of intending. By recognising the distinction between second and third levels of intending, one separates from Kant, for Kant would deny the self-transcending activity of reflective insight on sufficient evidence; he would deny that knowledge could be attained in respect of what was in fact so, beyond what was only thought to exist. Kant would not accept the notion of absolute objectivity!

3.1c Absolute objectivity

Wendice, using his wife's key to open the door to the apartment, betrayed himself by revealing that he knew where his wife's key had been hidden in the assassination conspiracy. The Inspector needed the concrete sense data of this experiment in order to verify what he had proposed. So, with Wendice here acting out his guilty knowledge, the Inspector was enabled to experience something new, an act of reflective insight, thereby reaching the absolute component of objectivity. By means of his reflective insight, he grasped that the conditions required to really link the hypothesis and concrete, experiential verifying conditions were fulfilled. This reflective insight combined both the experiential (first-level intentionality) and normative (second and third-level intentionality) components of objectivity.

His reflective insight consciously empowered him to grasp that now, having sufficient evidence in having his last final, relevant question answered, rationally he had to proceed to give assent, having to say yes to what his hypothesis had proposed: Wendice was responsible as the real architect of the assassination plot that had resulted in the killing of Swan.

This reflective insight and its judgement of 'yes', the absolute component, placed what was proposed by the hypothesis in its absolute realm. It was truly now beyond conjecture; it was now known fact that Wendice was guilty.

> But in the world mediated by meaning, objectivity has three components. There is the experiential objectivity constituted by the givenness of the data of sense and the data of consciousness. There is the normative objectivity constituted by the exigences of intelligence and reasonableness. There is the absolute objectivity that results from combining the results of experiential and normative objectivity so that through experiential objectivity, conditions are fulfilled while through normative objectivity, conditions are linked to what they condition. The combination, then, yields a conditioned hypothesis with its conditions fulfilled and that in knowledge is a fact and, in reality, is a contingent being or event.[70]

---

70   Cf. Lonergan, 2017, p.246, par.5, p.247, par.1; note confusions of naïve realist, naïve idealist, rigorous empiricist, absolute idealist, critical idealist stances etc.p.247, par.2

The reflective insight grasped that what the hypothesis had proposed was now absolute in that its conditions had been met, and an unconditioned, Lonergan says, is an absolute and, precisely as unconditioned, is not dependent on anything else or on any knowing subject. Grasping an unconditioned, one goes beyond subjectivity. Through reflective insight authenticating one to give assent, one steps into an absolute realm. 'There is nothing outside being that can take a look at it and have being as its object. If it is outside being, it is nothing. You move through judgement, through the unconditioned, to an absolute realm, and in that realm you find not only objects but also yourself.'[71]

Absolute objectivity alone can posit an absolute realm in which real distinctions occur. Indeed, as far as there being any bridge between oneself and an object, it can only happen through being absolutely objective! There is no other way of being absolutely objective than by attaining reflective insight.

How do we get to two real distinct beings? By judging: 'A' is, 'B' is, 'A' is not 'B'. If this is true, then in the absolute realm, there are two. If one of them is a 'knower' and the other is not, then one is the subject and the other is not a subject but an object judged. To say 'I am', one has to use transcendental method, experiencing oneself, understanding that experiencing and judging that understanding.

So, one knows oneself only if objectified; that is, if questioned by the questions pertaining to the transcendental notions, and by their respective answers. If the subject is not objectified, then as subject the subject is simply not known in the absolute realm. Only by proceeding in the objectification at the behest of the transcendental precepts can one divide up the absolute realm

---

71   B.Lonergan, 1990, p.172, par.3; p.174, par.1; Cf.1992, pp.407-408

into many objects, among which the subject and object can be known to be real and distinct.[72]

3.2 The triple cord of objectivity

So, again, we arrive at the triple cord of this objectivity. This triple cord comprized the experiential component, the normative component and the absolute component. We grasp, then, that the real is that which is intelligently grasped and reasonably affirmed in the data of experience. The third component, the absolute component of saying 'yes' to, or of giving assent to, what the hypothesis proposed, combined the previous two components of objectivity.

Importantly, we note that one component without the others could not attain objectivity. Again, in the world of immediacy it is enough simply to see and look and experience in order to know because, in the world of immediacy, the 'necessary and sufficient condition of objectivity is to be a successfully functioning animal'.[73] But in the world of the adult, by judging correctly, one adds absolute objectivity to the normative objectivity of understanding and reflection.

As Lonergan says: 'through experiential objectivity conditions are fulfilled while through normative objectivity conditions are linked to what they condition', and the combining of these two prior objectivities (experiential and normative) effects absolute objectivity where what is proposed has its conditions fulfilled 'and that, in knowledge, is a fact, and in reality, it

---

72 Cf. Lonergan, 1997, p.98, par.3, p99.par.1
73 Lonergan, 2017, p.246, par.5, p.247, par.1

is a contingent being or event'.[74] So, in the adult world mediated by meaning and motivated by value ...

> ... objectivity is simply the consequence of authentic subjectivity, of genuine attention, genuine intelligence, genuine reasonableness, genuine responsibility. Mathematics, science, philosophy, ethics, theology differ in many manners; but they have the common feature that their objectivity is the fruit of attentiveness, intelligence, reasonableness and responsibility.[75]

3.3 Objectivity is the fruit of authentic subjectivity

Again, responsibility is the new driving power (intentional notion) operative on the fourth level of intentionality, but it could only become operative when the intentional drive to know for fact, operative on the lower third level of intending, had been satisfied. Inspector Hubbard exhibited here the three levels of his intentional consciousness operating in a structural pattern of self-assembling, dynamic, conscious, mutual support.[76]

This accomplishment of ascertaining fact evoked in him the new intentional drive to be responsible becoming operative; and in virtue of this drive to be responsible, he could and had to proceed to go to the phone and ring the Home Secretary.

That procedure seemed to be second nature for Chief Inspector Hubbard. His subjective intellectual capacities in practice seemed to be accustomed to proceeding in this sublating orientation of his operative levels of conscious intentionality. This

---

74 ibid.

75 B.Lonergan, 2017, p.248, par.3

76 Cf. B.Lonergan, 1988, "Cognitional Structure', p. 207, pars.3-4. Prof. T.Daly defines the real as that which stands up to persistent questioning..

threefold process of self-transcending sublating cognitional activity resulted in the Inspector's knowing that Mrs Wendice was in fact innocent. He then knew her to be innocent independently of anyone's knowing.

The Inspector had been spontaneously faithful to the transcendental method. This spontaneous fidelity brought him to know the innocence that truly and really belonged to Mrs Wendice. His verification was indeed objective and that objectivity was the fruit of his authentic subjectivity:

> Before the subject can attain the self-transcendence of truth, there is the slow and laborious process of conception, gestation, parturition. But teaching and learning, investigating, coming to understand, marshalling and weighing the evidence, these are not independent of the subject, of times and places, of psychological, social, historical conditions. The fruit of truth must grow and mature on the tree of the subject, before it can be plucked and placed in its absolute realm.[77]

3.4   The pattern of transcendental method is unrevisable

In reflecting back over the line of the sequence of these actions (we are quite aware of not rushing to judgement before we have asked and answered all the relevant questions – just as did Inspector Hubbard), we notice very clearly that there stands out a unity in this sequence. A unity is obtained because of the drive to know that unfolds in ordered sequence of the prosecution of the sublating levels of intending that result in the unification of the transcendentals. We notice how consciously, and within the

---

77   B.Lonergan, 2016 (CWL 13) A Second Collection "The Subject" p.61, par.3

inner law of this aforementioned sequence, there is operating a dynamic, self-assembling pattern of these knowing operations that is fully conscious and spontaneous in each of us. We keep to this pattern, either in mere spontaneity by mere unreflective habit, or we keep to this pattern also by attending to it, by understanding its validity, by reflectively grasping its full reasonableness and by responsibly deciding to keep to the pattern. And in this case, we are critically and responsibly acting according to this pattern of knowing.

Actually, this spontaneous pattern is one that we can never put aside. It is a spontaneous pattern that alone we can use to revise any report or summary or objectification of the pattern. So, Lonergan says, the pattern is unrevisable, and the activities of the pattern occur, all right! Who could say he had never experienced seeing something or had never been aware of his own actions and so had gone around like a sleepwalker? Or who could say that he never once experienced being intellectually curious or obtained an insight or expressed what he caught onto? Who could say he never reflected on something to find if it was true or not, never judged anything in the light of evidence? Who could say he was never responsible in what he said and did?[78]

As for the pattern in which these operations occur, it is already present, operating spontaneously if we ask about something. We are then conscious we are trying to understand from relevant data, and we are not acting unintelligently. For an example, we know we gave some man ten dollars and we were owed five dollars in change. We want to understand what he did with the missing five dollars, and we are able to judge if what he says is reasonable or not. We just have to be critical; that is, reflecting enough to understand correctly if he acted justly towards us or not.

---

78   Cf. B.Lonergan, 2017, pp.20, 21

Before we judge, we wait for him to offer some intelligibility of any possible, omitted relevant question and answer, for when we judge, we are fully conscious we are wanting and asking for an explanation that can stand up to our persistent questioning. Only answers that carry sufficient intelligibility and reason will satisfy us.

We are conscious of this spontaneity of our taking in information or data, inquiring as intelligent and reasonable human beings. We are then unhappy in ourselves if we cannot reach a good conscience, of seeking that right be done and of seeing it done. We are conscious enough of this spontaneous pattern in our living, and it is normative in our conscious and intentional operations, no matter how well we or others can describe it or define it theoretically. Indeed, again, to attempt to revise this spontaneous pattern, one finds one has to use it. And then too, what would one be doing but revising a description or definition of the pattern, but not the spontaneous, real, dynamic, conscious pattern itself within us. So, we cannot really revise this spontaneous, self-assembling, dynamic pattern in our knowing and deliberative activities. It is then a rock on which one can build.[79]

The pattern involves an intellectual self-transcendence. We note here too the meaning of 'transcendence'. This intellectual transcendence is an intentional self-transcendence which is a:

---

79 "Obviously, revision can affect nothing but objectifications. It cannot change the structure of human consciousness." B.Lonergan, 2017, p.21 par.3. To revise, one must evaluate and choose responsibly in accord with the normative pattern of our operations. So having to use this pattern, one cannot revise it. For the pattern would be rejecting itself. So "There is, then a rock on which one can build. "The rock..is the subject in his conscious, unobjectified attentiveness, intelligence, reasonableness, responsibility." B.Lonergan, 2017, p.22, pars. 2, 3.

... coming to know, not what appears, not what is imagined, not what is thought, not what seems to me to be so but what is so. To know what is so is to get beyond the subject, to transcend the subject, to reach what would be, even if this particular subject happened not to exist ... Still, the self-transcendence of knowledge is merely intentional. With the moral a further step is taken, for by the moral we come to know and to do what is truly good! That is a real self-transcendence, a moving beyond all merely personal satisfactions and interests and tastes and preferences and becoming a principle of benevolence and beneficence, becoming capable of genuine loving. What, finally, is religion but complete self-transcendence? ... a radical being-in-love, a first principle of all one's thoughts and words ...[80]

3.5 Cognitional self-transcendence grasped by the intellectually converted is the clue needed for solving the critical problem

3.5a How do we get to know the real?

Knowledge of the real, Lonergan says, is not a knowing of some aspect or quality of a thing; rather, the whole of each thing is real:

... and by reality, we mean nothing less than the universe in the multiplicity of its members, in the totality and individuality of each, in the interrelations of all. To know the real is to know the universe. As our intellects are potential, so our knowledge of the real is a development.[81]

---

80   B.Lonergan, 2016, "Natural Knowledge of God", p.109, pars.3&4, p.110, pars.1-3

81   B.Lonergan, 1997 p.98, par.2

This development is obvious. One has to learn to be intelligent and to be rational and to be responsible. Lonergan points to the child's progress; he has to learn to distinguish between fact and fiction. The young person has to grow into wanting value and to constantly choose what is of value.

So, may we say, according to Lonergan, something is known to be real insofar as it can be experienced, understood and judged. Reality is the goal of questioning for our understanding and our judgement. Our capacity to know the real is our ability to grasp in our experience what a thing is through acts of insight and of conceiving and of judging if these particular items do in fact exist. All is real in that there is no item that could not come up for judgement. To know something is real is to be gained by following the same procedure for knowing anything and everything.

Here, Lonergan makes an invaluable contribution to a very old problem on what it requires for us to know truly 'what is'. To know what is real is not a movement from inside outwards as if we have to build a bridge for us to look at the object out there. (The old myth again: that knowing is like looking and that being objective is seeing all outside or inside that is there to be seen or intuited.) Rather:

> The critical problem … is not a problem of moving from within outwards. It is a problem of moving from above downwards, of moving from an infinite potentiality commensurate with the universe towards a rational apprehension that seizes the difference of subject and object in essentially the same way that it seizes any other real distinction.[82]

---

82   B.Lonergan, 1997, p.98, par, 3, p.99, par.1.

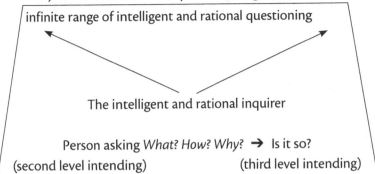

The reality of the universe in all aspects is intelligible within the infinite range of intelligent and rational questioning

The intelligent and rational inquirer

Person asking *What? How? Why?* → Is it so?
(second level intending)   (third level intending)

> 3.5b Knowing is not just by looking at something. All
> that is known – being and reality – is known only
> through true judgement.

Again, it is a matter of our being unlimitedly able to question intelligently what is experienced in order to understand what is experienced and, through the reflective act of understanding, to rationally judge and assent to what is so understood and conceived. This powerful spiritual activity of reflective understanding – say that of Inspector Hubbard, having waited for sufficient evidence – can grasp the distinction between Mr and Mrs Wendice as to who is really guilty. Also, as we have found with Inspector Hubbard, there is no substitute for knowing what is actually real other than by a reflective act of understanding, wherein we are rationally compelled to affirm or to deny the truth and so to know the real, existing distinction of anything at all from what is not real i.e. from what it is not.

To sum up, the real, Professor Daly says, is the object of all questions.

> 3.5c There is no item that cannot be known;
> everything that is intelligible is within the range

of the twin magnificent, cognitional activities of intelligence and judgement.

So, realism is immediate, but not in a naïve sense of being unreasoned and blindly affirmed, immediately given, unquestioned, perceptible and visible to the physical or some kind of spiritual eye. The universe is not real in the way the mouse is real to the cat as it excitedly anticipates the satisfaction of consuming the tasty morsel behind the panel in front – the mouse is already out there, now real for the cat – nor is the universe actually real as Halliday, upon just formulating his theory, exclaimed that he knew Margot was innocent.

But the Inspector corrected him, saying that only when that door opened would they 'then know everything!' Their hypothesis still needed the final question to be answered. This answer would be made by the presentation of the data of Wendice using his wife's key to open the door. Instantly, with this presentation of required experiential data, would occur the absolute element of objectivity by the Inspector now, with his final relevant question being answered, being able to understand he had met the conditions for giving assent to his hypothesis.

It is then that realism is immediate in that we know the real in this sense that, before we distinguish one real thing from another, or one subject from an object, we have the givenness, the data of inner or outer actuality as but 'the condition for the rational transition from the affirmation of possible to the affirmation of actual, contingent being'.

The givenness of data stimulates inquiry, and concepts stimulate reflection that allows rationality to demand judgement. This process is for every intelligibility, and what is real is subject to this process. And the real is as immediately available and present, not as a naïve realist would have it available for a good hard, long look, but as it is subject to the intelligent and reflective process just mentioned. So, a critical realist knows three things i.e. that:

> (1) ... the real is the concrete universe of being and not a subdivision of the 'already out there now real'.
>
> (2) ... the subject becomes known when it affirms itself intelligently and reasonably and so is not known yet in any prior 'existential' state; and
>
> (3) ... objectivity is conceived as a consequence of intelligent inquiry and critical reflection, and not as a property of vital anticipation, extroversion and satisfaction.[83]

We have noted Lonergan saying that being is what is to be known by the totality of true judgements. Apart from being, there is nothing. So, being is all inclusive. We therefore conclude that we can get to know the real because data are present for us to question intelligently and rationally. The real is as immediate as that which is present for processing intelligently and rationally. There is no thing that cannot be questioned; and merely looking at something does not suffice to make a thing real, nor is the real actually presented to us as answers; rather, the real universe is first presented to us immediately as data and as potentially knowable and is indeed to be questioned for understanding and judgement.

So, Lonergan notes, we distinguish between the infant's world of immediacy and the adult's world mediated by meaning. The infant relates immediately only to the objects it knows through sensing, but adults relate immediately to objects intended by their questions and known mediately by correct answering. In more technical language, these objects intended by adults are

---

83   B.Lonergan, 1992, p.413, par.3; cf. B.Lonergan, 1997, p.99, par.1

beings and adults seek to know them by inquiring what a thing is and by asking, 'Is it so?' and by finding correct answers.[84]

Again, indeed we might ask, 'Is the world real?' Well, whatever is real is not nothing; it is *something* and as such can be data for questioning for understanding and for judgement. To say something is real, then, is to recognize it has a place in that scheme of being assessed by experience, by understanding and conception, and grasped by reflective insight to be truly existing in its own right. Again, anything is real in that it has potential to be understood as a possibility and to be judged as existing in its own right, independent of anyone's thinking.

This scheme of assessment is universal and so, because of this existing potentiality as data for our intellectual and critical inquiry, the universe is real. So, to say anything is real is to assign it a place in that universal scheme.[85]

Again, simply, if we may, what we can question can be intelligible to us by the second intentional level of questioning for understanding – what, how and why? What is so conceived by such questioning for intelligence can be known by us through verification. This is where we ask third intentional level questions i.e. but is this so? Is it true? Is it real in terms of what we have understood and conceived about anything at all? All that can exist is immediately a possible object for our intelligent inquiry and critical reflection. All is in range already, as in the film, *The guns of Navarone*, where the German great twin guns commanded whatever was in the harbour. Only by negating those guns could the British shipping be out of reach. A team of Allied explosive experts was secretly sent for neutralising this

---

84   Cf. B.Lonergan, 2016, p.205, par.3; Cf. pp.204-206
85   Cf. B.Lonergan, 1997, p.98, par.2

firepower. By those guns and their great range, any shipping in the harbour was a given target within their firing range.

No being escapes intelligent inquiry and critical reflection and their supporting triple cord of experiential, normative and absolute objectivity. Let us take this imperfect analogy and imagine the harbour to be the universe of being. It was not that the harbour was too wide and out of range for the German guns. It was not. It was a matter of seeing to the proper exercise and care of those twin guns.

In summary, then, the pure desire to know, as Lonergan says, is unrestricted; it asks about everything, about being; that is, about all things. The capacity of the pure desire to know any concrete being at all comes about by constant proper inquiry through the sublating levels of intelligent and rational consciousness. Thereby, too, one is developing self-transcendence – cognitional, moral and religious.

Respecting that openness to the intelligible, to the true and to the good, by letting oneself constantly be driven along by the intentional notions and their questions on each level is to relate to that which is intelligible, true and good. And indeed, ultimately only God can satisfy the openness toward the infinite, by bestowing the gift of personal relationship with the Father, the Son and the Holy Spirit. Aristotle said it was hubris for man to want to be friends with God, but Christian revelation tells us that God the Father in Christ and their Spirit invite us into such friendship forever.[86]

---

86 The ultimate horizon intended by the unrestricted pure desire to know goes beyond the enlargement of horizon that is possible for the pure desire to achieve naturally. This happens beyond resources of "every finite consciousness, where there enters into clear view God as unknown, when the subject knows God face to face, knows as he is

3.5d Table: the universal pattern of operations of knowing what is true and of acting morally – transcendental method!

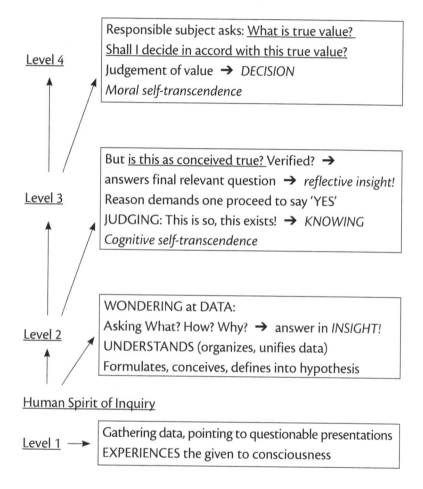

Level 4

Responsible subject asks: <u>What is true value?</u>
<u>Shall I decide in accord with this true value?</u>
Judgement of value → *DECISION*
Moral self-transcendence

Level 3

But <u>is this as conceived true?</u> Verified? →
answers final relevant question → *reflective insight!*
Reason demands one proceed to say 'YES'
JUDGING: This is so, this exists! → *KNOWING*
Cognitive self-transcendence

Level 2

WONDERING at DATA:
Asking What? How? Why? → answer in *INSIGHT!*
UNDERSTANDS (organizes, unifies data)
Formulates, conceives, defines into hypothesis

<u>Human Spirit of Inquiry</u>

Level 1 →

Gathering data, pointing to questionable presentations
EXPERIENCES the given to consciousness

known". This ultimate enlargement alone defines the final complete openness of the pure desire. This openness is given "as gift, as an effect of grace…as *elevans*, as *lumen gloriae*" B.Lonergan, 1988, p.187, par.3. For the reference to Aristotle .I am indebted to Prof.T. Daly S.J

3.6   Believing Chief Inspector Hubbard

One can choose responsibly to rely upon such a person as Inspector Hubbard who himself rigorously and persistently asked all the relevant questions. Through exacting experimentation, he clearly put his final relevant question so that his persistence yielded for him a reflective insight. He experienced his new reflective insight bringing him the full rational demand that he just had to proceed rationally and say, 'Yes, Wendice is guilty and the wife innocent.' He experienced the warranty consciously, so that to not proceed to affirm this would have been irrational. This allowed him to give his own immanently generated knowing as authentic witness to the Home Secretary.

The Home Secretary could responsibly accept this immanently generated knowledge gained by Chief Inspector Hubbard, for the Home Secretary had not the benefit of such immanently generated knowing as had the Inspector; the Home Secretary was not able to have the time or expertize to have presented to him relevant data, or to persist with raising relevant questions in regards to that relevant new data. Nevertheless, the Home Secretary could act responsibly by accepting the witness of such a creditable and recognized, credible investigator and so the Home Secretary could choose responsibly to proceed to affirm what the Inspector had affirmed.

The Home Secretary could make a judgement that believing is worthwhile and could affirm that the Inspector was a credible witness and that his witness here was worth accepting as true. Human affairs proceed this way. We would be reduced to primitivism, Lonergan says, if no one could take the responsible word of someone else. Then, in virtue of this value judgement, the Home Secretary could decide to accept the Inspector's testimony and make a reasonable assent and say, 'Yes, the husband is guilty and not the wife.' Here the Home Secretary knows by believing.

Believing is a knowing, a choosing freely to decide to give assent to something as true by authority of proper and responsible witness. Believing is different from the knowing that is immanently generated (a knowing by one's own experiences, understanding and judgement). Inspector Hubbard's knowing came about through his own extensive investigations on his three levels of intentional consciousness for all of which investigations enabled him to arrive at a reflective insight.

This reflective insight, by its own authority and by its own warranty of full rational power and reasonableness, generated the assent entailed: 'Yes, Wendice is the guilty party, not the wife!' The Home Secretary, upon judging the value of the Inspector's witness, decided to give assent to the innocence of Mrs Wendice. Lonergan would approve, for he says, 'Critically controlled belief is essential to the human good; it has its risks, but it is unquestionably better than regression to primitivism.'[87]

---

87   B.Lonergan, 2017, p.46, par.2

Chapter 4

The basis of Metaphysics: being is intrinsically intelligible. Critical Realism: the desire to know and self-transcendence in knowing and deciding get us to what is real

Cognitional self-transcendence and the critical problem

4.1 Our desire to know is the source of objectivity in our activities of knowing

When Inspector Hubbard first appeared at the door of the apartment where the killing had occurred, it was plain for all to see that he was a person wholly intent on a purpose. This understanding of him was confirmed by his immediate focus and his questioning of those in the room. The Inspector wanted to know two things: who was responsible for the dead man lying on the floor and why was he killed. He carried around a notebook and noted down answers relentlessly. He manifested an inquiring spirit. And he was not just content with noting down things that happened to come his way to experience; he was interested only in pieces of information that could be questioned for understanding on what had happened in regards to the killing. So, he selectively gathered his bits of information. He was assiduously carrying through his investigation into the killing of the man before him.

What he came to understand was again and again subjected to his further checking and critical questioning. His desire to know led him to seek adequate understanding through his self-correcting process of learning, for he raised further questions that brought him further insights both to correct what he thought and to complement what he had come to know for real.

THE DESIRE TO KNOW

pure, cool, disinterested, detached

Conscious drives intending to get to know (Transcendental Notions) expressed in sublating sets of questions: What? How? Why is it so? Is it true?
Value? Decide responsibly?

Transcendental Precepts:
Be attentive (notice)
Be intelligent (catch on? How do things fit, unify?)
Be reasonable (reflect, be critical and check theory; grasp reflective insight to give assent)
Be responsible (Value? Shall I decide accordingly?)

True Judgement: knowing what is, being, value

Choosing what is of value

4.2 Being is reality

The universal goals of Transcendental Method are the intelligible, the true and the real, and value. What is truly known is not an abstraction. For what is known is concrete, in that all about it is understood and affirmed to exist and so known to be real. So all of it belongs to what is being.

Being is the objective of the pure desire to know. Intelligent inquiry and critical reflection, intelligent grasp and reasonable affirmation have being as object. Being is precisely what is known by understanding correctly. So being is nothing apart from what is intelligible. Being is known completely when there are no further questions to be answered[88].

What is not being is nothing. What is known can be intelligently and rationally judged to be true in the relevant data. So our understanding and judging in sublation do attain to know what does exist. Our intelligent grasp and critical reflection intrinsically are apt to know something correctly: they are ordained to know being. And through intelligent grasp and critical reflection there is attained reflective insight that rationally demands one to give assent to what is proposed to be truly being so. No rational

---

88   "Now if by being one means the objective of the pure desire to know, the goal of intelligent inquiry and critical reflection, the object of intelligent grasp and reasonable affirmation, then one must affirm the intrinsic intelligibility of being. For one defines being by its intelligibility; one claims that being is precisely what is known by understanding correctly; one denies that being is anything apart from the intelligible or beyond it or different from it, for one's definition implies that being is known completely when there are no further questions to be answered". B.Lonergan, 1992, p.523, par.4

demand urges the mind to give assent to what is nothing: none can reasonably say, "yes, nothing is not nothing but something".

Attending to data, Lonergan says, gets us to know but a partial aspect of what could be real. Understanding brings us to know what it is that may or may not exist. Verification gets us to know that what understanding brings us in fact does exist, that this thing as understood with a particular nature in fact does exist. *So, all being is not beyond our understanding activity; all being is intrinsically intelligible.* What is understood is to be conceived, expressed, formulated and then assessed for judgment. The pure desire to know aims at knowing being not through incorrect understanding, but through correct understanding. "We conceive in order to judge"[89]. Inspector Hubbard could not rest until by answering the final relevant question he had verified that his hypothesis did propose an understanding that was correct.

And again, being is precisely what is known by understanding correctly. Intelligent inquiry and critical reflection, indeed all intelligent grasp and reasonable affirmation aim for or intend the goal of knowing being. And it is one's sublating experiencing, understanding and judging that intrinsically of themselves do gain for us correct knowledge of what is proposed. In this correct knowing one knows what is so, what does exist, being rather than nothing. Also, what is not nothing is truly real. Either something is being or it is nothing. *So then these activities of intelligent grasp and critical reflection also intrinsically demand us to affirm what is being and not nothing and so to affirm what is real. These activities bring us to know both being and reality.*

What is universally reliable is the dynamic knowing structure of conscious intentionality to know all being. The sublating unity of the knowing activities of intelligent inquiry and critical

---

89   Lonergan 1992, p.298, par.6

reflection attain whatever is to be understood and known in assent. The elements of whatever is to be known can be then defined according to this heuristic structure of knowing. So intelligibility is what is to be known by understanding; being is the object of the pure desire to know. All that is, is being. What is not being, is non existent or nothing. Intelligent inquiry and critical reflection are intrinsic to knowing being or anything that exists. What is not being is nothing and nothing has nothing and no data for understanding and so cannot be understood. So *clearly, reality is intrinsically intelligible; reality is what is to be known by intelligent grasp and critical reflection. Being and reality are identical.*

So then, as Inspector Hubbard would have been conscious of his mind's drive that was carrying him from sensing and imagining something to understanding it. Then this drive that he was conscious of did not stop at his gaining some idea of what had happened. No! Whenever he had attained some idea clearly he just had to question it to check to see if it could stand up to his persistent questioning. When it finally did so stand up, he became aware of something new, for he became then conscious he had fulfilled all the conditions his hypothesis demanded in order for it to be assented to. And then conscious of reason demanding him to, he had to give assent. Then he was aware that his drive to know had come to rest.

But the Inspector was not aiming for personal gratification and satisfaction as such in these activities. He purely and simply wanted to know the truth in the matter of the killing of Mr. Swan. Certainly, his desire to know gained satisfaction in getting to correct judgment. Certainly, he had been very clever in being so intelligent to pick up on Wendice being unaware of Swan putting the key back under the staircase carpet before entering the room. And then very intelligently and rationally he had set up the test for Wendice. But the Inspector was not thinking of or trying to be clever. He sought only to get results. So to this extent we can say the desire to know that he experienced was one that was "pure,.. cool, disinterested, detached", and it aimed wholly to get to know what is true[90].

And observing Inspector Hubbard, as we have noted in the previous chapter, one became aware of his operating according to a pattern of sublating self-arranging sets of questions that aimed for the goal of knowing what was true. One could gauge how he aimed consciously at his goal through his questions for intelligence and judging. Though of course, he himself was not expressly acting according to an explicitly formulated procedure. We have found in his coming to know the truth of Mrs. Wendice's innocence how there was operative in him a sublating self-arranging structure of partially knowing activities that united in a way that one further set of questions would take over and organize the answers of a prior set in a higher way.[91]

---

90 Cf. Lonergan 1992, p.373, pars.2&3

91 "...Answers to these and to any other questions have but a single source. They cannot be had without the functioning of the pure desire. They cannot be had from the pure desire alone. They are to be had inasmuch as the pure desire initiates and sustains cognitional process.... The fact that you ask, results from the pure desire. But to reach the answer, desiring is not enough; answers come only from inquiring and reflecting." Cf. Lonergan 1992, p.374, par.1. Cf. Also Ibid., p.374, pars 2 & 4; and Ibid. p.376, pars.1&5.

DESIRE TO KNOW ➜ BEING (objective of the pure desire to know)

> ➜ can question anything that is or can be
> can inquire intelligently and can reflect critically on all that is
> ➜ So, all that is is answerable to these questions
> All that is is then intrinsically intelligible
> *Being is intrinsically intelligible*

DESIRE TO KNOW ➜ BEING

> Cannot question what is outside of being – what is nothing
> Nothing can't question
> Nor can nothing be questioned
> *There is nothing to question*

Nor can there be judgment without prior understanding, nor understanding without experience. The proportionate object of human knowing not only is intrinsically intelligible but also is necessarily a compound of three distinct types of intelligibility[92] So any being, in that it is knowable is intelligible. Yet

---

92   "... the intelligibility known in understanding, it is the *formal* intelligibility that is the content of insight". But insight results from what we inquire into, so our understanding presupposes some presentations of what is to be understood, and such presentations are in some sense intelligible". The materials for inquiry to understand, and when inquiry reaches its term they are understood. Yet these presentations are of only *potential* intelligibility. It is not the intelligibility of the idea, of what is grasped inasmuch as one is understanding; it is the intelligibility of the materials in which the idea is emergent which the idea unifies and relates." Finally ...inasmuch as one grasps the virtually unconditioned one knows the intelligibility of the factual. While the potentially intelligible is what can be understood, and the formally intelligible is what may or may not be, the actually intelligible is restricted to what

the most fundamental question of all asks about existence. "If nothing existed, there would be no one to ask questions and nothing to ask questions about"[93]. Indeed, originally it is the intrinsic intending of our intentional notions of the transcendental method operative in our human knowing that enables our knowing to be intrinsically objective. And as one might well claim that being is known only by understanding correctly, one knows that being is nothing apart from what is intelligible, for one's definition implies that being is known completely when there are no further questions to be answered.[94]

4.3 The critical realist recognizes that it is the desire to know, the unrestricted intending through a process of self-transcendence that moves one towards the intelligible, the true, the real and the good

How does the intelligent, rational subject move from one transcendental level to the next? The intentional notions or drives demand us to ask questions that promote us from one level to the next. These questions express the transcendental notions that intend being. Questions for intelligence – what, why and how? – promote us from experiencing to understanding. Questions for reflection – Is it so? Is it true, real? – move us on to judgement, then we are aware of questions for evaluation and deliberation – Is this a value? Shall I decide accordingly? – that moves us from judgement to decision.

---

in fact is. In particular, proportionate being is what is to be known by experience, intelligent grasp, and reasonable affirmation. B.Lonergan, 1992, p.524, par.5; p.525, pars.1.&2

93 B. Lonergan, 1992, p.676, par.6

94 B. Lonergan, 1992, p, 523, par. 4

On the side of the same unity that is the subject asking the questions, many operations as parts, in sublating order of a functioning whole, are linked up. Answers unify into a single whole object known .On the side of the object, partial elements, gained by answers to the questions put by the intentional notions, are being unified and organized and are accumulating into a single whole. Thus, insight grasps the intelligibility of what sense perceives. Expression, or definition, or conception, or hypothesis unites what, separately, sense perceives and intelligence grasps; namely, the possibility, say, of Mr Wendice being the architect of the assassination attempt on Mrs Wendice, for insight reduces a mass of data into a single unity that can be clearly understood.

Unification of data is the primary element in insight, and this unity is put clearly in the one whole hypothesis. Insight holds all things at a point. Good is value, truth is what we assent to. God consciously understands God's self and all other things in perfect organization and unity. The oneness is infinite, Daly says, through infinite understanding and also, because it is complete understanding, therefore no further questions are required, so divine understanding is judging.[95]

Again, the drive to know moves one towards the intelligible, the true, the real and the good. People speak of concepts of being, even of the idea of being, and of affirmations of being, but Lonergan says people 'unfailingly' overlook 'the overarching intention of being which is not a concept nor an affirmation nor an idea".[96] He points to the utterly significant moment where this overarching intention through questions as to what, why and how gets

---

95   Prof. T. Daly, Lectures on Insight, Canisius College, 1995

96   B. Lonergan, 1988, p, 214, par.1

one to unify the data in insight or understanding and to make sense of data.

The exigent, imperious drive to insight! And when understanding is fresh, it is very much felt.[97]

Lonergan points to the dramatic incident of Archimedes in the moment of his discovery of a solution to a problem of how to test King Hiero's crown to see if it was of gold or not. Lonergan emphasizes that it was not so much that Archimedes had been bathing in the baths at Syracuse and his outburst of delight caused him to run naked through the streets in sudden, uninhibited exultation; rather, it was that it pointed to all the prior inquiry in its tension of labour and absorbing desire to get to a solution and that this tension was released in the getting of the insight answering the problem. Archimedes certainly had that desire. As a result, he got the insight to weigh the crown in water to see if it was of pure gold. He grasped a central insight into the principles of displacement and specific gravity. This point unified through intelligible organization the data to be understood.

> Deep within us there is the drive to know, to understand, to see why, to discover the reason, to find the cause, to explain ... the fact of inquiry is beyond doubt ... It can demand endless sacrifices ... what better symbol for this obscure, exigent, imperious drive than this man naked, running, excitedly crying, 'I've got it!' And insight comes suddenly and unexpectedly.[98]

---

97   Cf. B.Lonergan 1992, p.28, par.3

98   B. Lonergan, n, p, 1992, pp.28 -29

4.4 Sublating intentional notions unify the intelligible, the true, the real, the good

Insofar as an object can be questioned for understanding, verification and decision, it is within the range of investigation for intelligibility, truth and reality and worthwhileness. These result from the sublating questionings of the levels of intentionality. So, the transcendentals – the intelligible, the true, the real, the good – are unified! They all come from the one source; namely, the drive to know that carries all the intending of the intentional notions throughout the dynamic structure of knowing. This drive to know also relates these four intentional notions and their respective levels of inquiring in a unified organization and in an integrating sublation, as noted earlier:

> ... for the intending subject intends, first of all, the good but cannot do so without knowing it to be real; to know it to be real, he must know what is true; to know what is true, he must grasp what is intelligible; and to grasp what is intelligible, he must attend to the data of sense and to the data of consciousness.[99]

So, one cannot understand one's own conscious knowing activity if one separates understanding and conceiving from judging. Instead, if one attends carefully to one's own operations, one grasps that 'conception unites what separately sense perceives and intelligence grasps'.[100] One too is aware that once one spells out an idea clearly, one is not just satisfied to stop there. One has to inquire further with different questioning to

99 B.Lonergan, 2016 p.108, par.2
100 B.Lonergan, 2016, p.108, par.2

verify one's hypothesis, for 'we conceive in order to judge'.[101] And judging can take place once the intending subject reflectively understands that the final relevant question has been answered in the required concrete data, so fulfilling the condition remaining for the idea proposed by the hypothesis to be verified. In doing this, one understands that one has then met all relevant conditions set in order to proceed to give assent. So, too, one cannot separate but rather must grasp the unity between the intelligent intending through understanding and the rational intending for judging fact and the moral intending for what is of true value. The rational assent of fact is sublated by the moral judgement and responsible decision, so that the intending subject chooses rationally and responsibly what is good and loving.

There is then a real unity of the human spirit through means of the drive to inquire and know, sublatingly operative throughout the levels of intending set by the intentional notions of the dynamic structure of knowing.

Again, intentional self-transcendence is a continuity in operations through cumulative results. One gets to know, not what appears to be so, nor what one imagines to be so, nor what one may think to be correct, nor what seems to one to be true, but it is one's going beyond oneself to know what is in fact the case, or what is so, through one's correct judging of one's understanding. So, one's intentional self-transcendence is intellectual in that it is intelligent and rational self-transcendence, for the knowing subject is going beyond herself or himself to reach the object to be known that exists as an intelligibility and identity in its own right. Indeed, the knowing subject knows being i.e. what is intelligibly one and possible, what is true, what is real and what is of value.

---

101 B. Lonergan, 1992, p.298, par, 6

Knowing correctly sublates into moral self-transcendence. Also, one needs to know correctly what is the right thing to do. One can then choose correctly and so transcend oneself morally. That is, instead of acting unreasonably only to please oneself, one rather acts responsibly by choosing and acting in accord with one's correct judgement of value, doing what is truly and objectively correct. One comes through judging what is the good and right thing to do, to know what to choose correctly and so then to be enabled responsibly to do what is good and right.

Choosing to act this way as a rule, we achieve real moral transcendence of ourselves, for we regularly and constantly leave aside what brings us personal gratification and satisfaction of taste and of self-interest in order to become benevolent and beneficent. So, too, we become able to share genuine love with others[102].

For the critical realist, cognitional activities that occur in sublating order obtaining on one's four conscious levels of intentionality attain to what is real. So, then the world, mediated by meaning and motivated by value, is the real world. This is because the critical realist realizes that the process of experiencing, understanding and judging and deciding is truly a process of self-transcendence.

4.5　The world mediated by meaning and motivated by value[103]

102　Cf.B.Lonergan, 2016 "Natural Knowledge of God" p. 109, par.3.

103　Cf.B.Lonergan, 2017, p.75, "There is a systematic exigence that separates the realm of common sense from the realm of theory." 2017, ibid, p.78, par, 5.;cf.2017, Ibid p. 79, par2. Also, there is a "realm of common sense and a realm of theory" Ibid, p.80, par2. Eddington's two tables, Ibid.2017, p81, par, 3. And too, note, "Differentiated consciousness appears when the critical exigence turns attention upon

4.5a   The realm of commonsense meaning

A father takes his young son to the zoo.[104] 'Look out, Dad, the notice says that it spits!' The young son is wondering about the giraffe's possible attitude to them, if the animal would turn on them and spit at them. The boy would not want to disturb the animal. What is being spoken about? What is the boy thinking of? He is focusing on how the giraffe will react to or relate to them. The animal has such a long head and it could lean a good deal in their direction and fire its missile at them. So, the boy is concerned with how the giraffe will relate to them and with how they will relate to the giraffe.

How will the boy come to know the giraffe? He will carefully note just how it will behave towards them. He will keenly remember just how they will be acting towards the animal. If, say, the boy were to call out to it, or even wave a flag at it, he may find out if it is friendly or unfriendly. He will try something out by behaving towards the animal in certain ways. He will get some insights into how to attract it or how to alienate the animal. So, he will get to know the animal by a succession of insights he will have and which will give him a growing knowledge on how best to act and to get along with Mr Giraffe. He will correct his own ideas by getting new insights into what works and into what does not promote friendliness with the animal.

His learning will consist in a growing number of new practical insights. He will eagerly undertake this self-correcting

---

interiority, ..."Ibid. p.81, par.3. , Finally, "one can move beyond the realms of common sense, theory, and interiority and into the realm in which God is known and loved" 2017 Ibid, p.81 par.2.and cf. pp.75-82

104   Cf. B.Lonergan, 2017, p.79.par.1. I have elaborated on Lonergan's reference to the boy with his father at the zoo.Lonergan, 2017, p.80, par.1

process of learning because he likes the animal and wants to get along with it. The boy will reach a point where he will have a pretty good working idea of how to befriend the animal, that will put him in good command of the situation and enable him to judge fairly well what will work and what will not work in getting along with giraffes.

The boy will be using his ordinary, everyday language to speak of his friend the giraffe and of how it relates to him and of how he relates to it.

We use our common sense to speak of this everyday world with its objects that interest us; in fact, we call it a commonsense world. Words in this commonsense world do not point to intrinsic properties of things. Instead, words in commonsense world language aim to get us to focus our intentionality on the objects of our interest in this everyday world. In commonsense language, we make our attitudes clear to these objects, our expectations of them, our own intentions towards them, our own understandings of them, our own judgement and decisions towards them. From our practical experience of these commonsense world objects, we speak of what they might intimate to us, of how they understand us and of how they might feel towards us and act towards us.[105]

4.5b The realm of theory

Meanwhile, the father has been standing there but not listening

---

105 Cf.B. Lonergan, ... 2017, "The realm of commonsense.".p.79, par.1; "The systematic exigence not merely raises questions that common sense cannot answer but also demands a context for its answers, a context that common sense cannot supply or comprehend. This context is theory..."ibid., p79, par.2

much to the boy's observations and excitement, for the father is a zoologist. Although he has been looking at the same giraffe, he has a far different interest in the giraffe. The father will have been noting how the animal's peculiar inner systems combine and interlock. That long neck. He just wonders and stands in awe at how it functions in its 'skeletal, locomotive, digestive, vascular and nervous systems', and how these, from the neck down, interlock with those systems of the rest of the animal's body. The father's words will be naming, not what helps him and his son to be friendly towards the giraffe and the giraffe friendly towards them, but instead the father will be using words that name the intrinsic properties of those interlocking systems operative within the giraffe as it walks, stands and moves. Being a zoologist, the father is a scientist, and in his biology he will have special words to denote particular, carefully defined parts of the giraffe's skeletal, locomotive, digestive, vascular and nervous systems.

Now, as we elaborate on the example Lonergan gives, we may relate that the boy simply might not be able to keep up with the words the father is using, for example: 'skeletal', 'locomotive', 'digestive', 'vascular' and others.

The boy asks, 'Dad, is that big word, "loco ...", saying something about the giraffe being brought here on a train?' The boy has no idea of what dynamically organising elements are connecting and functioning and interrelating within the animal, nor has he yet learnt that these big terms his father has been using have been developed over a long period to denote fittingly precise, interrelating functions within the body of the giraffe. Such new terms the boy never hears of in the street, playing soccer. All his father's words seem to belong to a new world that is home to the inner relatings of the interior functions of the animal. These are terms that are not used in everyday speech because only biologists, like his father, use these scientific terms since they alone are interested in the inner relatings that go on within the nature of this animal and of all giraffes as such.

So, the boy begins to recognize that his father belongs to two different worlds. The father lives with him and his mother in the everyday world, the world of common sense where they know what works for them and what helps them to live humanly in wellbeing and peace with each other and others. And then his father lives at the laboratory with his science friends in their world of theory, of highbrow investigation. Also, they have their own language that they use in speaking with each other. But there in the laboratory, they are more interested in the general ways inner elements of animals 'get along' (one could say 'interrelate', but the young lad may not happen to use such a word).

Similarly with the chemical periodic table. People ordinarily do not speak of these chemical terms unless they are working in chemistry, teaching and researching. Also, as questions grow, these scientists order their answers in a helpful progression, or in an intelligible line of inquiry concerning the interrelatings within the nature of things being examined. For example, inorganic chemistry deals with the preparation and the properties of the elements and compounds etc. and, continuing further, oxides are classified into acidic and basic oxides, neutral oxides and peroxides. The basis of the modern description of the elements is the periodic table. The elements are arranged in the order of increasing atomic weight, or more correctly, in the order of atomic number. The context here is theory.

To objects referred to in the realm of theory, Lonergan says:

To these objects one can ascend from commonsense starting-points, but they are properly known, not by this ascent but by their internal relations, their congruences and differences, the functions they fulfil in their interactions[106].

And he goes on to note that 'Mass, temperature, the electromagnetic field are not objects in the world of common sense'.[107]

So, where common sense is a viewpoint from which we consider things in their relation to us, science is a viewpoint from which we consider things in their relations to one another. The boy's father will speak to visiting biologists and be able to take up any topic in zoology, even though his visitor comes from another country, for they speak the same scientific language.

The father's friend is from Bavaria, next to but not Austria. He comes from a little village outside Munich. There are local customs there that are different from those in other places, yet the visiting zoologist still gets along so well with his father. They immediately can get along, talking all the time about things in biology that interest them. They seem to be talking about things that anyone anywhere, indeed anywhere in the whole world, who is interested in biology could understand. They seem to be talking on universal topics and using a language that has very technical terms for things. They all know exactly what each person there is referring to, because the terms that they use carefully and exactly stand for the objects they intend to deal with. His father and his friend from Bavaria do not talk about poetry or how they get along with other people so much, but rather his father and his Bavarian friend talk about things they are mainly interested in. These things are impersonal and are called by very technical words and have relationships that can exist anywhere and at any time.

---

106 B.Lonergan, 2017, p.79, par.2

107 B.Lonergan, 2017, p.79, par.3, p.80, par.1

4.5c The desire to know, and to live in the world mediated by meaning and motivated by value

A striking example of a human being's desire to know, and to live in the world mediated by meaning is when Helen Keller's teacher took Helen out to the yard to a pump and water and let the water flow over Helen's hands. The teacher made a sign for 'water' on Helen's hand and Helen, after some time, happened to catch on. She gained a momentous insight, affecting her whole life, that this sign made on her hand by her teacher, was referring to the water. From that moment she connected this finger sign on her hand with the name for water. So, this is what happened for Helen; that she then got an insight into how a sign could be used to convey a meaning.

Helen Keller's sudden and most exciting insight here was that a certain succession of touches on her hand, signs made by her teacher, conveyed the names of objects. Helen was profoundly moved and with deep emotion, she put question after question to the teacher. She got down on the ground and asked the name for 'earth' and the emotion she experienced begot an intense interest inside her. She immediately signified her desire to learn the names of about twenty objects in a very short time.

Lonergan refers to this moment of the discovery of language. By using language, he says, meaning finds its greatest liberation. It is not that early humans prized words in that they supposedly conveyed the essence of a thing; rather, they prized words because by means of words, they thereby activated or brought conscious intentionality into sharp focus so they could then intelligently focus upon their world, eventually to find some intelligible organization in it. So, they could understand, judge what was worthwhile and decide how to live in it.[108]

Chief Inspector Hubbard lived in a world that was dependent principally upon the questioning of relevant data of experience, of sense and of consciousness. He first inquired, noting in his notebook data he had gathered of which he could ask questions for understanding what, how and why. These latter questions resulted in his experiencing insights that he clarified into clear expression and eventually into hypotheses. So, Inspector Hubbard was not a naïve realist; knowing, for him, was not just having a good look but rather, asking questions and waiting to be able to judge. That is, with this reflective insight he carried out the triple cord of objectivity completely. He unified the components of experiential and normative objectivity with an absolute objectivity.

This insight would therefore be the high-point that would sublate his prior insights that gave him his hypothesis and his weighing of evidence. This high-point would be the concrete component of Wendice finding his wife's key and opening the door with it, so verifying the Inspector's ultimate hypothesis.

Reality, then, is not just simply the world in which infants speak, a world of immediacy. The criteria for reality in the world of immediacy are that you are able to perform the activities to see, hear, taste, smell, touch, feel, enjoy or suffer: that seems all you have to do to get to what is real. This world of immediacy is:

> of sights and sounds, of tastes and smells, of touching and feeling, of joys and sorrows. But as infants learn to speak, they gradually move into a far larger world. It includes the past and the future as well as the present, the possible and the probable as well as the actual, rights and duties as well as facts. It is a world enriched by

---

108 B.Lonergan, 2017, P.68, pars.1, 2

travellers' tales, by stories and legends, by literature, philosophy, science, by religion, theology, history.[109]

But the criteria for reality in the world mediated by meaning not only include the activities of immediate experience but much more. One has to act according to the transcendental precepts and to proceed by the transcendental notions and to attain to the triple cord of objectivity. And importantly, as we experience a reflective insight, we gain an answer to our final relevant question that enables, in our consciousness, an emanating, correct judging.

Throughout his inquiry, Inspector Hubbard was seeking meaning for what had happened, and he would not be satisfied until, on the third level of intentional consciousness and reasonableness, he got to the true meaning of what had happened that referred to what existed no matter who knew of it. He was seeking absolute objectivity. In fact, he was driven by the intentional notions to transcend himself cognitively and get to what truly existed beyond his own activity.

Also, Inspector Hubbard now had to face up to questions for being responsible. He just had to question responsibly what was of value in the newly discovered fact of Mrs Wendice's innocence and had to responsibly come to judge her innocence to be of true value and so to be worth appropriate, responsible honour and action for vindication. He also could not avoid the moral attraction and responsible compulsion emanating from his correct judgement of the value of Mrs Wendice's innocence i.e. that he proceed to decide to ring the Home Secretary on her behalf. So, by his being of upright moral consciousness, he proceeded further to act responsibly in good conscience.

Inspector Hubbard was acting in a world mediated by

---

109 B.Lonergan 2016, "The Origins of Christian Realism", p.204, par.1

meaning and motivated by value. It was beyond the world of immediate experiencing. His world was certainly not one in which he just had to wait for meaning and value merely to be given to him.

> Over and above what is given, there is the universe that is intended by questions, that is organized by intelligence, that is described by language, that is enriched by tradition. It is an enormous world far beyond the comprehension of the nursery.[110]

So, understanding and judging and evaluating and deciding, in addition to the reception of data of sense and to data of consciousness, provide a new world of meaning and of value. This new world is of meaning and of value in addition to the world that is merely sensed and imagined and perceived. The world of meaning and of value that is intended by questions – intelligently organized, motivated by value and opened up by language and tradition and known by correct answers – presents itself for our inquiry as an enormous universe. This enormous universe far outstrips the world that empiricism and neoplatonic idealism promise us. In this universe lives the critical realist who discerns:[111]

---

110 To the infant something is real if the infant can see, hear, touch, taste, or enjoy or suffer it. The criterion whether it is real or not is for the child immediately to experience something. But for the adult one requires also to go beyond merely experiencing, to understand what is relevant, so as accurately express it and to judge what it is correctly. Cf. B. Lonergan, 2016, p.204 pars.1-3

111 To Lonergan, "Critical" means one can distinguish between the world of immediacy and the world mediated by meaning. For the critical realist, "critical" means that one rejects the intuitive account of knowing,

In this universe lives the critical realist who 'distinguishes between object and objectivity in the world of immediacy and... object and objectivity in the world mediated by meaning and motivated by value'. So then for such a person objectivity is simply 'the consequence of authentic subjectivity, of genuine attention, genuine intelligence, genuine reasonableness, genuine responsibility.'[112]

---

that knowing is by taking a look at something. Rather, one is "critical" if one grasps that knowing by judging in the self-transcending process, distinguishes the second from the third level of conscious intentionality of judging, and attains cognitive self transcendence. Therein one seeks reflective insight from which emanates the rational demand to proceed to judge. To know is to act in this critical way. Also, "Only the critical realist can acknowledge the facts of human knowing and pronounce the world mediated by meaning to be the real world; and he can do so only inasmuch as he shows that the process of experiencing, understanding, and judging is a process of self-transcendence." Lonergan, 2017, p224, par.2.

112 B.Lonergan, 2017, p.248, par.3

Chapter 5

Intellectual, moral and religious conversions

5.1 Chief Inspector Hubbard's investigative mode that manifested an openness to and capacity for intellectual conversion

First, the Inspector diligently questioned data presented throughout the whole criminal investigation. What did these data mean that were being presented to him? Second, he arrived at insights and carefully worked out their intelligibility into thoroughgoing expressions in theories. Third, with these hypotheses so conceived, he went on to reflect on them by not resting until he had reached a theory that finally stood up to his persistent questioning. He so arrived at the truth of Mrs Wendice being innocent, an innocence that stood independently of, and so as a reality transcending, all the Inspector's inquiring through experiencing, understanding and judging. By keeping faithful to the demands of objectivity throughout in raising and answering the questions proper to the intentional notions, he had come to truly know the reality of her innocence.

Such was Chief Inspector Hubbard's wont. He would not give assent to something being so or true until he had persistently asked and answered all relevant questions. Let us note that he had not, in theory, worked out in any set of technical terms and in a universal manner his turning away from that stubborn myth that knowing is like looking and that being objective is seeing all that there is out there to be seen. To turn away from that idea on knowing and objectivity towards the idea that knowing requires experiencing, understanding and judging is a turning around that Lonergan has called 'intellectual conversion'.[113] Although he had not formally addressed being so converted, in practice he acted according to the dictates of this intellectual conversion, so that for Inspector Hubbard, in fact and in practice though not yet perhaps elaborated in theory, the true and the real was neither something immediately given through experiencing or visibly to be looked at nor something merely apparent, nor something to be taken for granted, nor just the bright idea alone, nor merely the possible, nor the merely rational, nor the suasively emotional but in point of exercise and fact, the real and the true was the verified!

If he could then understand and verify for himself – from his own very conscious, self-assembling, dynamic, intellectual pattern – he would know the real was that which he was intelligently grasping and reasonably affirming in the data of his experience.[114] He could be brought to grant perhaps that to reach the

---

113 Lonergan affirms the need for "intellectual conversion": so one has to reject the *"myth" that knowing is like looking, that to be objective is to see what is visible, that to find what is real is to see what is out there now.* But this is a myth, he contends, that refuses to recognize that the world of immediacy "the world of the infant" is quite distinct from the world mediated by meaning, where to be objective we experience, understand, judge and believe, and so find what is real. B.Lonergan, 2017, p.223, par 4 , p.224, pars. 1, 2

114 A compound object of knowing is constructed by uniting several elementary objects, and this is achieved by the work of transcendental notions. Cf. B.Lonergan, 2017, p.224, pars 2,3; also B. Lonergan, 2016, A Second Collection, *The Subject*, p.61, par.3; Lonergan,1988,p.211,par.3,212,par.1

self-transcendence of truth, the subject has to undergo the slow, laborious process of being taught, of learning, of investigating, of coming to understand, of testing and weighing the evidence. Also, he could be brought to appreciate that such activities are not independent of the conscious subject, of time and place, of human conditions that are social, psychological and historical: 'The fruit of truth must grow and mature on the tree of the subject, before it can be plucked and placed in its absolute realm'.[115]

'Empiricism, idealism and realism name three totally different horizons with no common identical objects'. That is, realists do not restrict themselves only to operating on the first level, or merely on first and second levels of intentional consciousness. Instead, realists work on all three levels in sublation.

Lonergan goes on to note that the aforementioned types of philosophies work within different horizons and that they deal with goals that have nothing in common. 'An idealist never means what an empiricist means and a realist never means what either of them means'. We might add here, to distinguish an empiricist from other naïve realists, for the empiricist an object could only be what is sensed and for the idealist, the object could only be what is thought and sensed, and for both the empiricist and idealist, the real is what is immediately given in experience. For the critical realist, the object of inquiry could be whatever is intelligently grasped and reasonably affirmable in the data of experience. 'For the critical realist, a verified hypothesis is probably true, and what is probably true refers to what in reality is probably so'.[116]

For example, Lonergan asks, what are historical facts? The empiricist, who thinks reality is already out there now to be looked at, would answer that historical facts are out there and capable of being looked at. The idealist thinks out some theory based on discovered documents to reach, at most, only

---

115 B.Lonergan, 2016, A Second Collection, "The Subject" p.61, par.3

116 B.Lonergan 2017, p.225, par.1

a mere thought of the mind. The critical realist, however, by getting to true judgement on what is understood from discovered data, reaches facts of history. She or he would also discern theories understanding courses of events according to their being credited with higher or lower degrees of verification of probability. In fact, very many people, as they begin to speak of knowing, of objectivity, of reality, already take it for granted that only by having a good look at something can they know it. But now, Lonergan says, to be liberated from this blunder, one has to learn to identify one's cognitional activities at work on their respective levels of conscious intentionality in a process of self-transcendence when one is seeking to know something. Indeed, one can break from the long-ingrained habit of naïve, realistic thought and its consequences, Lonergan reminds us, by taking time to experience the self-transcendence knowing demands. And again, this self-transcendence one begins to understand as one, in one's own experience, identifies and verifies the distinct kinds of activities one is doing when happening to act on the distinct, sublating levels of conscious intentionality. Then, on personal experience and understanding and reflection, one can judge that knowing is not the same as merely looking at something, nor is doing the right thing a matter of just gratifying oneself.

So, in all, one has to ask the questions (what, how and why? Is it so? And is it of value? Shall one decide according to this value affirmed?) that belong to the intentional driving notions in order to reach what is intelligible, what is true, what is real and what is good. These questionings bring one into the world mediated by meaning and motivated by value, way beyond the world of the nursery (level one activity) where knowing is just merely to experience something immediately. This is why exercises and puzzles of experiencing insights are so valuable and are recommended in references below:[117]

---

117 B. Lonergan, 1988, " p.209. par.1

5.2   A critical realist recognizes one proceeds on all three levels in sublating self-transcendence in order to know what is real

Level 3 Judging	Critical realist: experiencing and understanding and judging Theory verifiable? → *reflective insight!* → 'YES' World mediated by meaning is the real world, because it can show the process of *experiencing, understanding and judging is a process of self-transcendence.* Know reality by the correct answers.
Level 2 Understanding	Naïve realist: world mediated by meaning known by looking, or by a kind of spiritual looking. Idealist: only the immediate experiencing of sensing gets one to know the real world, yet understanding gets one to know an ideal reality. Critical idealist: Only by sense intuition can one know anything. Understanding can refer to objects only if it refers to data of sense. And so one never knows the real thing itself.

Level 1
Experiencing
	Immediately experiencing data: to see, to hear, to look at etc. suffices to know.
	Naïve realism: real if given in immediate experience.
	    Knowing is taking a look, objective if seeing all that is to be seen.
	    What is out there can be taken for granted as being real.
	World mediated by meaning known but only
	    by a kind of looking; real if presented, experienced even though unquestioned.
	Objective knowing only through senses' activities, or by sensible intuition.
	Empiricism-naïve realist:
	    World mediated by meaning, not known reality at all: understanding, conceiving, judging only subjective activities, not objective.

... for the world mediated by meaning is a world known not by the sense experience of an individual but by the external and internal experience of a cultural community, and by the continuously checked and rechecked judgements of the community. Knowing, accordingly, is not just seeing; it is experiencing, understanding, judging, and believing. The criteria of objectivity are not just the criteria of ocular vision; they are the compounded criteria of experiencing, of understanding, of judging and of believing. The reality known is not just looked at; it is given in experience, organized and extrapolated by understanding, posited by judgement and belief.[118]

Let us summarize, then (see diagram above). A naïve realist is convinced that by an immediate experience such as looking at something, he could know the world that is mediated by meaning. An empiricist holds he knows something to be objectively real as long as he can sense it or imagine it. He holds that sense experience or imagination are then his only criteria for being objective and that consequently, understanding and conceiving, judging and believing are merely subjective activities. An idealist would maintain that as well as sense experience of an object, one can understand that object, while one would yet agree that what is real can only be that which is sense experienced, so that the world mediated by meaning is not real but ideal.

5.3   Intellectual conversion

As one comes to turn away from those worlds of naïve realism, of empiricism and of idealism, one turns to the world mediated by meaning and motivated by value, to the world of the critical

---

118   B.Lonergan, 2017. P.224, par.1

realist. One undergoes an intellectual conversion; that is, one undergoes a radical shift from thinking that to get to know something, one has to have some kind of a good look at it and one casts off the conviction that to be objective about anything, all one has to do is to have a good look at it out there and to see all that is out there to be seen. Instead, one now realizes in a startlingly new way that knowing is by the conscious, sublating, dynamic, self-assembling structure of those four levels of intentionality that are set up by the intentional notions issuing from the pure desire to know.

> Knowing is not just seeing or looking. Knowing is experiencing, understanding, judging and believing, and the criteria for these are threefold criteria for objectivity. The reality known is not just looked at; it is given in experience, organized and extrapolated by understanding, posited by judgement and belief.[119]

A critical realist is one who has been intellectually converted. For her/him, cognitional activities that occur in sublating order obtaining on one's four conscious levels of intentionality attain to what is real so that the world mediated by meaning and motivated by value is the real world. And this is because he or she realizes that the process of experiencing, understanding, judging and deciding is truly a process of self-transcendence.[120]

Inspector Hubbard may not have had that experience that Augustine had when Augustine, at a point in time, suddenly grasped that reality did not have to be only bodily. He was then turning away from that stubborn myth that knowing is like

---

119 B.Lonergan, 2017.p.224, par.1; cf. ibid. pp.223-225
120 Cf. B.Lonergan, 2017, p.224, par.2

looking and being objective is seeing all that there is out there to be seen; a conversion, noted above, that Lonergan has called 'intellectual conversion'.[121]

If we may stress the effective, practical example of Inspector Hubbard: for him, in fact and in practice though not yet perhaps elaborated in theory, in his investigations the true and the real was neither something immediately given through merely experiencing or through something being merely visible to be looked at, nor was the real something merely apparent or intuited, nor something to be taken for granted, nor just the bright idea alone, nor merely the possible, nor the merely rational but in point of exercise, the real and the true was the verified!

Indeed, if he had put his mind to it, in his practice and from his experience, he was well in a position to determine what each cognitional operation specifically and exactly was and how each exactly related to and was defined in relation to the other cognitional operations. So, having focused just on these very operations in action together in their conscious, self-assembling, dynamic, unifying intellectual pattern operative in his very mind, he could then understand and verify for himself – from his own very conscious, self-assembling, dynamic intellectual pattern – that he was truly a conscious identity for whom the real was that which he was intelligently grasping and reasonably affirming in the data of his experience.[122]

Has one been stopped short by this new understanding of what is real? Or does one think something is real because one can just sense it, see, hear and touch it? Or that something is real merely because it is given to one in one's immediate experience

---

121 Cf. B.Lonergan, 2017, p. 223, par.4; 2017, p.224, pars.1-2

122 Cf.B.Lonergan, 2017, p.224 pars. 2, 3; p.225.par.1 Cf. B.Lonergan, 1988, "Cognitional Structure", p.207; cf. B. Lonergan 1992, chs.9-11

of it? Or simply because one can imagine it, it therefore has to have reality, so that the imagined is the real? Or that unless something has a reality that can be imbued with sensible qualities and has to take up a certain space and co-extend with a duration in time, it cannot be real? Or that merely thinking out a very clever explanation of things gets one to what is real?

Without raising and answering all the relevant questions, Halliday might go on to protest, out of his love and past knowledge of Margot, that he knew she was innocent and so take her innocence for granted, but the Inspector simply could not do it! As the Inspector said, only when that door opens and Wendice walks in using his wife's key, so furnishing the final piece of experiential evidence for his hypothesis, could he then grasp that he, with full reason, could give assent to her innocence.

The Inspector did not go on to explain how he had to experience a reflective insight in which he would grasp that all the conditions would be met for him to proceed rationally, and by rational cogency under pain of being consciously irrational, to give assent to what his hypothesis had proposed. Even though he might not use these terms, as he had not formally raised the questions for his interiority as he could not speak in the technical terms of interiority, he intended to wait upon that cognitive event that a critical realist would call a 'reflective insight'.

5.4   What is moral conversion?

Indeed, Inspector Hubbard had been driven in reflective insight to transcend himself cognitively to say, 'Yes, Mrs Wendice is truly innocent.' Then because of this new proceeding judgment he made, he found himself driven responsibly now to transcend himself morally; namely, firstly to assent to the value of her newly found innocence and secondly, to decide to act in accord with that value judgement and do the right thing quickly by ringing the Home Secretary on her behalf.

In technical terms, the intentional drive to be responsible could be expressed in his case as this: because of his judging her innocence to be truly of value, should he be responsible and choose in rational accord with that value judgement to ring the Home Secretary? Should he truly tell of the objective finding of Mrs Wendice being innocent, for this phone call would liberate Mrs Wendice from execution. Indeed, he experienced a drive to be responsible and so to acknowledge the correctness of value to choose what was morally right and good to get her set free.

He then acted because of the transcendental precept – be responsible. Before he had acted in accord with the prior transcendental precepts – be attentive, be intelligent and be reasonable. Now he went straight to the phone.

Accordingly, Inspector Hubbard was changed. He had not only grown in true knowledge, but he had also truly matured in responsibility and in moral excellence. He had gone beyond what he was. He had transcended himself not only cognitively but morally as well. Well could he take time to take out his comb and spruce up his moustache.

Until he proved she was innocent, he could not recognize the personal value of her being innocent and so he did not feel obliged to act as if she was. Without the rational fullness of a reflective insight demanding him to proceed to give assent to her proposed innocence, he was not in a position to judge morally and to act responsibly in this case. As soon as he knew for the first time the guilt of Wendice and the consequent innocence of Mrs Wendice, the Inspector now experienced in himself a clear awareness of a pressing demand to be responsible and to ring the Home Secretary immediately.

He was to carry out this demand in two steps. From his reflective insight into the vindicated innocence of Mrs Wendice, the Inspector was aware of a new intending towards value, now operative in his consciousness. He could now judge very well that her vindication and her being set free were of true value. So, he experienced a responsible moral pressure so strongly attracting him that he first judge what value is to be assented to and secondly, that he decide to do all he could to honour the value of her vindicated innocence.

Now we can grasp how central and pivotal was his reflective insight into the fact of her innocence. We can grasp how, from that pivotal reflective insight (occurring with Wendice's opening the door) and its warranted judgement of the value of her innocence, there now also emanates a demanding responsibility that he proceed to act on her behalf.

In summary, one is intellectually converted if one is no longer convinced that merely by looking at something out there that one can know it; rather that only by experiencing, understanding and judging does one get to know something. One is morally converted if instead of merely acting from selfish reasons, one chooses constantly and of set purpose to act in the right way.

As we have grasped, Inspector Hubbard brooked no opposition to his getting to the truth, and only upon gaining his reflective insight did he know Mrs Wendice was truly innocent and only then did he absolutely respect her as being a person innocent of the killing. Then he could decide and did so to get her set free.

Inspector Hubbard, it well seemed, always acted this way, following out the demands of being rational and responsible. As he persisted in this moral conversion (we suppose he has been like this for a long time), he insisted only upon what was truly verified as of real value. This brought him to be conscious of a responsibility against bias wherever he found it. He was not a man to permit any shutting out of relevant data, or neglect of persistent, intentional questionings. So it was that he was intransigent in asking all the relevant questions until he could arrive at the reflective insight of absolute objectivity. His fidelity to do what was right protected his quest for what was true and real. And so his moral conversion sublated his intellectual conversion.[123]

Again, where before he may have wished her innocence proven, Inspector Hubbard was detached from any personal desires compelling him to rush to judgement of the value of her innocence. He sought only to be compelled by rationally proven fact. Nor was he aware, before he had experienced reflective insight which occurred with Wendice opening the door, of being responsibly driven to affirm her innocence. It was only upon this reflective insight that the Inspector in all honesty became conscious of being drawn by a new, strong, intentional force of responsibility, for then he was acutely aware he had to act responsibly to get her set free.

5.4a   Jean Valjean

Jean had escaped from prison where he had been brutalized. In his convict clothes, Jean was kindly received by the bishop. Indeed

---

123 Because each of the three conversions, religious, moral and intellectual, exists by means of self-transcendence, all three can relate by sublation which Lonergan defines ...Cf. B.Lonergan. 2017 p.226.par.3., p.227. pars.1-3.

Jean had become a desperate person, intent only on survival and for the most part having no regard for the rights of others. During the night, he had been thinking of the silver plates he had seen in the house, and early in the morning, he absconded with these only to be apprehended by the constabulary. He is then brought back to the bishop for identification. True to the sign over his door, 'A guest has come, it is Christ who has come', the bishop welcomed Jean, 'But you forgot a couple of other pieces that I gave you.' This occasion of Jean's experiencing extraordinarily kind love brought about in him a moral conversion experience.

Later we find that Jean, with the money he acquired for the silver that the bishop had given to him, has established a factory for the poor in the village, and later he makes them shareholders. What Jean puts first in his life is the value of helping others find employment and a living and new hope in life. Instead of spending the money on a mansion for himself, or on gambling, or on some other pleasurable and vainglorious satisfaction, Jean instead chose to seek the value of helping others reform and to find a good living for themselves. He so kept to this that he was appointed mayor, for his integrity, kindliness and unselfishness were universally admired.

So, we see in Victor Hugo's striking story an example of a moral conversion. From being a hopeless, brutalized criminal thinking only of his own need and satisfaction, he became a generous, kindly benefactor, not out for revenge but seeking only to promote value and to make the town a worthwhile place to live in for those in need. Hugo presented in Jean Valjean a moral conversion in dramatic and clear terms. Instead of selfish gain, Jean Valjean now judged it to be of paramount value to be helpful to others. According to this altruistic motivation, he decided to lead his life and never flinched from doing so.

In appreciation, Jean came to judge it worthwhile to accept

and to adhere to the true value of what had been done for him. Jean judged, as a deep personal value, the human reality of the bishop acting in such kindness towards him. As he himself experienced such goodness, Jean's own responses to human values were strengthened and refined so that he himself began to exercise his freedom in an ever advancing thrust towards authenticity (faithfully adhering to the transcendental precepts: be attentive, be intelligent, be reasonable, be responsible). He discovered for himself that his choosing to do what was right and good and gracious did wholly affect him. This authenticity did not allow him to be satisfied with anything less than this new, self-giving life for others.

He could now choose to let this bishop's kindness affect him more than had the brutalization he had suffered. So it was that when it came time to choose between, on the one hand, siding with the punishing, merciless application of the law by the chief of police towards a poor woman and on the other, showing her mercy, he did not bend to the threats of the new heartless, biased chief of police.

Again, it became most clear, when there was the imminent danger of a poor man being crushed by a wagon, that Jean risked his being detected as a long-escaped convict by this police chief. Jean had to choose between, on the one hand, risking being discovered as an escaped convict and, on the other hand, rescuing a poor farmer from being crushed by a cart that had fallen on him. Jean chose to rescue the poor farmer by using his exceptional physical strength that had been well known in the prison quarry where the chief of police standing nearby had formerly been in charge.

So it was that Jean had been morally converted, for he now opted regularly, naturally and spontaneously for the truly good and for value over mere personal satisfaction.

Jean continued to carry out actions that expressed his decision for value over his personal satisfactions. He even found he had to be responsible and to decide for good in order to save his enemy police chief from execution by the Paris rebels. Jean also came to be open to admit to a bias that had crept in towards his ward, making himself overly protective of her and separating her from the young man she loved.[124] But his openness to doing good to others eschewed this bias that was harming his process of moral self-transcendence. He then came to know he was shutting out the intelligibility of the good of the young couple's relationship. He grasped and affirmed the value that his bias had been preventing him from recognising and acting upon. So, he rescued the young man.

5.4b Moral self-transcendence

One could say that if moral knowledge is the proper possession of morally good people, then such a person as Jean Valjean merited that title, and one could be assured that what he decided and carried out would have been morally good. Jean Valjean was one who could not be at ease without choosing what was of value over mere self-satisfaction. He was morally converted.[125].

> Fourthly, by deliberation, evaluation, decision, action, we can know and do not just what pleases us but what truly is good, worthwhile. Then we can be principles of benevolence and beneficence, capable of genuine collaboration and of true love. But it is one thing to do this occasionally ... It is another to do it regularly, easily, spontaneously ... It is finally, only by

---

124 Cf. B.Lonergan, 2017, p.52, pars.2-4; p.204, par.3

125 Cf. B.Lonergan, 2017, p.225, par.3, p.226.par.1

reaching the sustained self-transcendence of the virtuous man that one becomes a good judge, not on this or that human act but on the whole range of human goodness.[126]

Also, where Aristotle spoke of the virtuous person, we might say Lonergan spoke of the morally self-transcending, converted subject and we might find an example of one such person in Jean, the one who was so open to, and practised in, checking biases and in constantly choosing value over selfish satisfaction. Jean was so practised in choosing what was of value, and in enacting that value, that he not only happened to choose what was good but that which he chose to do could be taken as a criterion of value .

The transcendental notion of consciously drawing the subject to be responsible and to seek value, sublates the prior three levels of intentional consciousness. The subject is very aware of being responsibly driven to judge value and to decide to act in accord with the value judged. In so deciding will the subject experience a happy conscience instead of an uneasy one.[127]

So, in summary, the path to this final step of moral self-transcendence begins as one's overarching intentionality draws one to, firstly, consciously inquire of data; secondly, to grasp what is a possible intelligibility and to conceive this in a concept or hypothesis; thirdly, to reflect on this hypothesis in order to judge; and fourthly, to be responsible to know what is of value and to decide responsibly.

So, it is the self-transcending benevolent (wanting to do right generously) and beneficent (doing right generously) subject who is able to collaborate with others and to love truly. It is in

---

126 Cf. B.Lonergan, 2017, p.36, par.2.; p41, par.3.
127 Cf. B.Lonergan, 2017, p.35, par.4; ibid.p.36, par.1.

sustaining this moral self-transcendence regularly and spontaneously that the conscious subject becomes virtuous.[128]

5.4c Between judgement of fact and judgement of value are intentional responses to value (feelings)

In the judgement of value, Lonergan states, three components
unite. First there is knowing what truly is really human; secondly,
there occur feelings, intentional responses to values, that happen between the judgement of fact and the judgement of value.
Feelings, as Lonergan says (and we have had something to say
on feelings in chapter two) are intentional responses that greet
the '... value of a person or the qualitative value of beauty, of
understanding, of truth, of noble deeds, of virtuous acts, of great
achievements'.

We are so endowed that we can raise questions for understanding and knowing till we gain cognitive self-transcendence
in correct judgement, but we can also be moved in experiencing ourselves drawn on the fourth level of deliberation. If we
may interpret Lonergan here, by intentionally responding, in
some deliberative way of deciding, to the possible value in
an object, this we name a 'feeling response'. By this feeling
response, 'we glimpse the possibility or the actuality of moral
self-transcendence'.

Thirdly, there is the judgement of value from which the drive
to be responsible leads one to correctly deciding in moral self-
transcendence; however, if the correct judgement of value is
lacking, the prior intentional responses to the object may not
turn out to be fine feelings after all. Such feelings are then shown

---

128 Cf. B.Lonergan, 2017, p. 36.par.2; p.41, par.3

to be of moral idealism and to not be real, 'lovely proposals that don't work out and often do more harm than good'.[129]

Then, too, true moral feelings have to be cultivated, for even loyalty can be felt as thieves work together and share the spoils of robbery. Wendice and Swan felt a certain loyalty of one to the other in their unjust and evil contract, but morally converted persons will seek to discern through correct value judgement. If they constantly act by correct judgements of value, they form habits to spontaneously aid themselves to choose value instead of what is merely self-gratifying. So, feelings have to be educated, refined, criticized. One so makes of oneself an authentic human being.

In this way, one's constant choices in moral self-transcendence groom one away from unauthenticity. One becomes aware of how important it is for one to judge value and to feel of such personal value and to choose and to act responsibly.[130] And when one falls in love, one's loving takes over and one's moral love of intimacy, of family, of neighbour are nourished by one's being in love with God.

One is growing in one's knowledge and acting humanly as one responds more to what are vital, social and cultural values – and so more to personal and more to religious values. Then, too, develops an openness to ever further achievement. At the summit of this ascent, 'there are to be found the deep-set joy and solid peace, the power and the vigour, of being in love with God'.

Lonergan then adds that inasmuch as one's love of God is supreme ('complete') then 'values are whatever one loves'. One, understands Augustine, loves God, and one may do as one so

---

129 Cf. B.Lonergan, 2017, p.39, par.2.
130 Cf.B.Lonergan 2017, pp.39-40; p.225, par.3; p.226, par.1

loving will be pleased to do. 'Affectivity is of a single piece. Further developments only fill out previous achievement. Lapses from grace are rarer and more quickly amended'.[131]

5.5   Religious conversion

Aristotle said it was hubris for man to aspire to be friends with God, but in one outstanding case, Paul's experience is telling us something different, for he says, 'For all who are led by the Spirit of God are children of God ... When we cry, "'Abba' Father!", it is that very Spirit bearing witness with our spirit that we are children of God'.[132]

Anyone who responds to God, as God offers friendship, experiences an utmost change in one's self-transcending sublation of one's intentionality. Such a person experiences a fulfilment of all one's intending on the four levels of conscious intentionality. God can offer friendship, and a 'being-in-love', to anyone whom God creates. One can respond because of the openness of one's dynamic, self-assembling structure of conscious intentionality ultimately to goodness unlimited. One becomes conscious of God's offer as one is drawn to understand correctly and to affirm value and to choose to act by this judgement. And one will be conscious of it at some time, though one may not know it is being made!

We understand this because we know now that being conscious is not yet knowing. Indeed, Paul tells Timothy that God wants all people to be saved and so God offers friendship even to those who speak and act as if God is not. Being saved means to accept the offer of this friendship with God. Also, those feelings one has that are of first importance are those that come from one's religious conversion where one is conscious of being enabled, without

---

131 Cf. B.Lonergan, 2017, p.40, par.1; p.100, par.5; p.101, pars.1-3.

132 Rom. 8:14-16 , NRSV. Cf..B.Lonergan, 2017, pp.102 – 103

knowing it, to act and to be in friendship with God. From this love, one becomes conscious of feeling deep joy and peace. So, then, one can be gifted to arrive at desiring to befriend the supreme value of God but may not know it. One keeps and nourishes this friendship if one tries to live according to correct moral values.

So, moral conversion is sublated by the fulfilment of religious conversion where one becomes gifted to be a 'subject-in-love', and one is 'held, grasped and possessed, owned through a total and so an other-worldly love".[133].

God's love sets all else in perspective. Inasmuch as one loves God, one wants only what God wants, and whatever God wants is a true value. So, Augustine could say, 'Love God and one may do then as one pleases'. Why? Because in loving what is of supreme value, one loves only what unites with supreme value, and so one conforms all one's desiring and evaluating and deliberating with that which is supremely worthwhile.

The consciousness, Lonergan says, that accompanies the subject's conscious deliberating and making judgements of value and deciding and acting responsibly and freely can undergo a religious conversion. Religious conversion affects the subject's level of conscious deliberation. This religiously converted deliberation becomes a basis for choosing that can be enlarged and enriched but not superseded.

Those who are religiously converted are then like those who are able to choose, judge, decide and act with an easy freedom to do good. And this 'at-easeness' and facility in habitually doing good flows from the fact that they have fallen in love. 'So, the gift of God's love occupies the ground and root of the fourth and

---

133 B.Lonergan, 2017, p.228, par.2

highest level of man's intentional consciousness. It takes over the peak of the soul, the *apex animae*'.[134]

This gift of God's love, flooding the soul, Lonergan says, is also denoted by the term, 'sanctifying grace'. Indeed, the gifts coming with this love poured in are peace, patience, kindness, generosity, faithfulness, gentleness and self-control.[135]

The term, sanctifying grace, Lonergan notes, belongs to the world of theory. Our terms come from the world of interiority. When we speak of the dynamic state of being in love with God, we speak from that stage of meaning where we find the world of interiority able to explain explicitly and clearly how the world of common sense relates to the world of theory. Also, in this world of interiority, it is fitting that the gift of God's love be first described as an experience (and on this point, Lonergan is refreshingly clear). It is only then that it can be objectified (questioned, understood and defined) in theoretical terms.

Consciousness, as we have seen above, is not knowledge, and knowledge is the fruit of the tree of the conscious,

---

134 B.Lonergan, 2017, p.103, par.1

135 Galatians 5:22 All these are identical responses to the value of being in love with God and of loving to be one with God in Christ. They are celebratory feelings that help mould a person's psyche and aid in a critical stance in regards to one's sensitivity and pre-waking consciousness. These feelings aid one, may we say, in one's psychic conversion, helping one to discern those feelings that promote the movement for human living and fulfilment. R.Doran adds a psychic conversion, which our short introduction to Lonergan does not allow us to expound. Cf. R.Doran, What is Systematic Theology? University of Toronto Press, 2005, p.111, par.3.

self-transcending subject by understanding his/her experience and judging that understanding to be correct.

God's love comes as a gift. Let us take the very clear example of Saint Paul. We might apply Lonergan's thought to get some minimal understanding of Saint Paul as he cried out, 'Who are you, Lord!' Paul, though not knowing it (for he had not as yet questioned data for understanding and come to verify his notion of what had happened for him), was conscious of being gifted to unreservedly give himself in love with the divine. Later he could come to a fuller understanding of the nature of his religious conversion. Paul became able to name the one whom he found unreservedly loveable as the Jesus Christ who in loving had captured him.[136]

Religious conversion is, we might say, this enlargement, enrichment and heightening of the fourth level of intentional consciousness that is the completion of 'the rock', spoken of above. Again, this rock is, '... the subject in his conscious, unobjectified attentiveness, intelligence, reasonableness, responsibility'. One experiences that unrestrictedly being in love is the proper fulfilment of one's capacity for self-transcendent intending and unrestricted questioning, for as Paul found himself suddenly converted to God in Christ, he found himself gifted to be unreservedly loving God in Christ. He found henceforth that unreserved loving to be the touchstone of all that he valued and of all that caught his interest and desire and knowing. Being in love, choosing to let himself be carried along in the love of God pouring into his heart, as it were, brought his fourth level of intentional consciousness to a peak. Being in love with God in Christ fulfilled Paul's conscious intentionality.

The eye of this love and interest, stemming from his decision

---

136 Cf. Phil. 2:12.

to live that way, affected the whole range of his interests and all his decisions. Faith, this eye of love, influentially secured ever more firmly the sublating of the first three levels of Paul's conscious intentionality. Also, this influence of uppermost loving brought forth an openness to the intelligible, to the true, to the good and loveable. Paul found himself experiencing a fulfilment:

> If anyone else has reason to be confident in the flesh, I have more. Circumcised on the eighth day, a member of the people of Israel, of the tribe of Benjamin, a Hebrew born of Hebrews; as to the law, a Pharisee; as to zeal, a persecutor of of the Church; as to righteousness under the law, blameless. Yet whatever gains I had, these I have come to regard as loss because of Christ. More than that, I regard everything as loss because of the surpassing value of knowing Jesus Christ, my Lord. For his sake, I have suffered the loss of all things and I regard them as rubbish in order that I may gain Christ and be found in him, not having a righteousness of my own that comes from the law but one that comes through faith in Christ, the righteousness from God based on faith.[137]

These are words of absolute decision and commitment in unreserved loving. This loving ensured freedom from biases to question without hindrance for intelligent inquiry and reasonable affirmation. Paul's fourth level of intentional consciousness was securely grounded in being loved unconditionally and in loving unconditionally in return, and this religious loving promoted the transcendental desirings (notions) for what is intelligible, true, responsible and loveable. This converted fourth level was his touchstone sublating all his valuing and

---

137 Phil. 3:7–9.

knowing in the light of his supreme valuing and knowing of God in Christ.

This converted fourth level was the culmination of 'the rock' of one's conscious intentionality above mentioned.[138]

5.6 Religious conversion sublates moral conversion, and moral conversion in turn sublates intellectual conversion

In religious conversion, 'one's affectivity is of a single piece'. All one's affection and desiring is in full perspective and totally whole. Whatever developments further occur only fill out prior achievement.[139]

Fourth level intentional consciousness is that which accompanies deliberating and which accompanies making judgements of value, deciding, acting freely and responsibly, but in religious conversion it is this deliberative consciousness that is led to a fulfilment. This fulfilment is such that this converted, deliberative consciousness is now a basis that may be developed and enriched but not replaced by anything better. It is a basis from which the conscious subject is ready to deliberate, to judge, to decide and to act freely with ease, as they who, from being in love, do whatever is good.[140]

By intellectual conversion, one transcends oneself to know how to attain that which is true, and what is true is so independently of one's own activity. It is then real. By moral conversion, one is enabled to affirm what is of true value, as against

---

138 Cf.B.Lonergan, 2017, p.22, par.3; also cf. p.102, pars.2, 1-4

139 Cf. Lonergan, 2017, p.40, par.1

140 Cf. B.Lonergan, 2017, p.103, par.1

selfishness and sole gratification, and to enact that value in one's choices and actions in real self-transcendence.

But religious self-transcendence is where one decides to accept the offer to surrender oneself to being a subject in love totally, and the one whom the consenting subject is conscious of surrendering to in total love is the one whom the conscious subject is experiencing as unreservedly good, loveable, true, intelligent and intelligible. The religiously converted person experiences the ultimately loveable as one who fulfils all one's intentionality and as one who demands the converted to nourish the sublation of one's constantly seeking the intelligible, the true, the good in one's process of self-transcendence.

So, religious conversion sublates moral conversion and moral sublates intellectual, for in accord with this total being in love with the one who unrestrictedly is of value and of truth, one orientates one's life to be a subject converted morally and intellectually (at least in practice open to intellectual conversion). Being in love unreservedly, one needs and is driven to live in good conscience, uniting with the one who is unreservedly loving, good, true and intelligent. Paul, for example, exhorts the Philippians to put on the mind of Christ, loving Christ as did.[141]

> And all three conversions can occur in the same consciousness.
> So, it is possible to conceive of these three conversions interrelating as a sublation.[142]

---

141 Cf. Philippians ch.2:3

142 B.Lonergan, 2017, p.227 par.2, " ... that what sublates goes beyond what is sublated, introduces something new and distinct, puts everything on a new basis, yet so far from interfering with the sublated or destroying it, on the contrary needs it, includes it, preserves all its proper features

So, moral conversion promotes one to proceed on from cognitional to moral self-transcendence. When Inspector Hubbard got to the fact of Mrs Wendice's innocence, he was driven by his responsibility to ask what he ought do about it. In this he experienced being driven on beyond fact to judging correct value and to choose responsibly and rationally in accord with that value. One so becomes an originating value. But this promotion did not prevent in any way the Inspector's cognitional self-transcendence. He was in no way less desiring of truth; rather, he was responsibly sublating and supporting his desire for correct judgement.

One is all the more desiring of knowing what is possible and true, real and responsible if one is driven notionally, intentionally to recognize what is of value and to be able to decide in accord with true value. One has to responsibly carry on one's persistent questioning in accord with the exigencies of rational consciousness. Indeed, that one does continue to do this is only strengthened because moral conversion arms one against biases.

Inspector Hubbard persisted in all relevant questioning without fear or favour, and that one is now within the context of seeking value and to enact value, one finds the need for truth only greater because one desires true, real value of oneself and for others.[143] Also, their religious conversion empowers them

---

and properties and carries them forward to a fuller realization within a richer context."

143 In moral self-transcendence, one becomes an originating value, and as such , needs truth for beneficence and benevolence 'for he must apprehend reality and real potentiality before he can deliberately respond to value.'. Cf. B.Lonergan, p.2017, p.227, par. 3.

more and more to value and to choose what is true and what is worthwhile and loving of God and of neighbour.[144]

Finally, the eye of religious loving – faith – reveals a value in believing the truths taught by religious tradition. In this tradition, one can say that the possibility of intellectual conversion is promoted, for in this tradition is preached the word of God, and in this preaching, the word of God is spoken and heard. That is, to commit oneself to be faithful to the word of God preached and heard requires much more than just physical seeing something with one's eyes, or just some spiritual seeing. To be faithful to God's word requires the whole person engage with the word, a whole engagement being where one is engaging all one's levels of intentional consciousness, to understand the word, to give assent to it, to value it. Being receptive to God's word also requires one to be open to being morally and religiously converted.

For a Christian, the eye of religious loving prizes being possessed by God's word revealed in Christ, and to value being in love, being captured by God in Christ as was Paul.[145] It requires one to be open to at least being a dogmatic realist, affirming to be true the preaching of the Apostles and the affirmations of the believing community, such as the definitions of Nicaea, Constantinople I, Chalcedon, and Constantinople III.

It is important to note that convictions and commitments rest on judgements of fact and on judgements of value and that these rely very much on beliefs. Believing plays such a large role in what people judge to be true, and the way believers present a

---

144 Cf. B.Lonergan 2017, p.103, par.1; also p.228, pars, 2&3.

145 Cf. Lonergan, 2017, p.228, par.4; Phil.2:12

solid front is by nourishing in themselves the conversions – religious, moral and intellectual.[146]

---

146 Cf. B.Lonergan, 2017 , p.230, par.2.

Chapter 6

One historical arrival at dogmatic realism contained the seeds of critical realism

6.1 Tertullian's naïve realism and his empiricism

At this time was being asked the question as to whether Jesus could receive the divine worship that was being given to the Father. It was a question as to whether Jesus had the very same divinity that the Father had. Nicaea will introduce a term, consubstantial, which means the Son has the same divinity with the Father. Tertullian (d. 220) meant to defend that the Son, in being born of the Father, was also of the same matter, truly and really fully divine. For this purpose, Tertullian offered comparisons or analogies that could be known by our senses. That is, he used sense-based analogies. For example, he pointed to how the root brings forth the shoot and to how the spring brings forth the stream and to how the sun brings forth the beam. So, one can see visually and imaginatively how the substance of the shoot or of the stream or of the beam is of the same stuff as is their source.

Yet one could ask Tertullian, for each example, is it not the case that what proceeds or emanates could be physically separated and exist independently with its own new, existing, independent substance? And so, the offspring could possibly arise with its own separate substance which in this case would be divine and a new divinity? The examples then do not quite fit what they wish to represent; namely, the monotheism of the one indivisible, divine substance of the triune divinity. Does not the oneness of God demand that there be no more than one divine substantial existence?

So, we find that Tertullian's empiricism in analogies could lead to division and multiplication of the Father's divinity and so could not suitably image how the one divinity of the Father by generation was also in the Son.

Tertullian's universe, Lonergan remarks, was to be thought of as being bodily. Everything had a body. Everything was in some way material. His mind is tied to images. The Son is other than the Father because he is a substance emitted, or extruded, from the Father's substance.[147] So, following Lonergan's lead here, we gauge that for Tertullian, to know was in some way to imagine, or to take a look at what had a body. Indeed, to rely upon sense experience and imagining; that is, to act merely empirically, for Tertullian, was to be objective.

---

147 Cf. Cornelius O'Donovan, The Way to Nicaea, Darton Longman &Todd, London, 1976, p.46, par.2

6. 2   Diagram: naïve realism (empiricism, idealism, critical idealism), dogmatic realism, critical realism

Level 3 Judging	Critical realist: experiencing and understanding and judging Theory verifiable? → *reflective insight!* → 'YES' World mediated by meaning is the real world, because it can show the process of *experiencing, understanding and judging is a process of self-transcendence.* Know reality by the correct answers. Dogmatic realist: reality known through judgement of believing, but reality believed is also imaginable, immediate. Mixture of naïve realism.
Level 2 Understanding	Naïve realist: world mediated by meaning known by looking, or by a kind of spiritual looking. Idealist: only the immediate experiencing of sensing gets one to know the real world, yet understanding gets one to know an ideal reality. Critical idealist: only by sense intuition can one know anything. Understanding can refer to objects only if it refers to data of sense. And so one never knows the real thing itself.

Level 1
Experiencing
	Immediately experiencing data: to see, to hear, to look at etc. suffices to know.
	Naïve realism: real if given in immediate experience.
	    Knowing is taking a look, objective if seeing all that is to be seen.
	    What is out there can be taken for granted as being real.
	World mediated by meaning known but only by a kind of looking; real if presented, experienced even though unquestioned.
	Empiricism-naïve realist: objective knowing only through senses' activities, or by sensible intuition.
	    World mediated by meaning, not known reality at all: understanding, conceiving, judging only subjective activities, not objective

But Tertullian did not have the advantage of the above grasp of the triple cord of objectivity. In fact, he was not emancipated from naïve realism. He, in practice, held that the first experiential component of objectivity sufficed for the object of inquiry to be placed in its absolute realm. For example, he held that the angels and the archangels and even the Son himself are not without shape, without a body, though the bodies that they have are not like those found on Earth; yet, he said, they are not unsubstantial beings that have no body. Their body is a spirit, but 'even a spirit is itself a body *sui generis*, for the things we call invisible have their own shape whereby they are visible to him'.[148]

Also, Clement of Alexandria said that the eye with which the angels see is not an eye of sense; it is the eye of intelligence, given by the Father, a spiritual eye.[149] For the naïve realist, as Lonergan says, the real is what is given in immediate experience whether it is the immediate experience of what is found either by sensing or by some intellectual perceiving with a spiritual eye.

> Knowing ... is a matter of taking a good look; objectivity is a matter of seeing what is there to be seen; reality is whatever is given in immediate experience. Such is naïve realism. Its offspring is empiricism.[150]

6.3   Origen's idealism

Origen (d. 254/255) was an advance upon Tertullian's empiricism. He insisted upon the Father and the Son being strictly immaterial, transcending the level of the senses. He eschewed

---

148 Cf. O'Donovan 1976, p.44, par.2

149 Cf. O'Donovan, 1976, p.115, footnote 18

150 B.Lonergan 2016, "The Origins of Christian Realism", p. 204, pars.4, 5

those expositions that relied upon 'absurd fables' of 'extrusions from the Godhead that some people pictured to themselves'.[151] 'For the Son was born like an act of willing from the mind' and did not separate from the Father, not because he was conjoined as is an extrusion to the material substance that emits it; oh no, but the Son remains one with the Father because the Son perpetually contemplates the Father's profundity'.[152] So, it is by a spiritual, immaterial looking that the Son gazes upon the substance of the Father and in this looking unites with that substance.

That is, the Son's generation did not proceed in the manner of human or animal generations. Instead, for Origen, the Son is the image of the Father and he proceeds from the Father as a decision proceeds from the mind, as implied in the text: 'Whatever the Father does, the Son also does'.[153] For the Son to know, then for Origen, was for the Son to be able to contemplate, to gaze spiritually upon what could be gazed upon. Cognitional objectivity resulted from this spiritual gazing. The divine profundity was known to be real because it could be gazed upon. Here, then, we note a naïve realism in Origen in that knowing consisted in the immediacy of a spiritual looking.[154]

The empiricist, however, discards the world mediated by meaning. Instead, for the empiricist, immediate sensible experience is the touchstone! Understanding and judging are of no use. Understanding is empty in that what it gives can be of value only if objects are sense given; but, we note, if we have access only to objects sensibly presented, we live in a world only of appearances – phenomena.

---

151 Cf. O'Donovan Ibid.p.58, par.2

152 Cf. O'Donovan, Ibid. p.137; p.59, par.6

153 Cf. O'Donovan, Ibid. p.59, par.1

154 Cf. O'Donovan, Ibid.p.59, pars.3-4

The critical idealist lives in a world of ideas. He accepts a contribution from understanding but does not recognize judging. Yet for the realist, dogmatic or critical, it is in judging that the knowing subject transcends itself to know what is independently real of its knowing.[155]

6.4 The break from empiricism and idealism to dogmatic realism

At the Council of Nicaea in 325 AD, the Nicene Fathers and those defending the full divinity of the Son, were defending in accord with what had been taught by the Apostles and their successors and by the practice of the believing community. They held to be true that what the Apostles taught was apostolic dogma (teaching) affirmed for communal belief; that is, they were dogmatic realists.

We note three things about dogmatic realists. Firstly, because they held as true what they were taught for belief as the Word of God, God's Word, they believed, is a true word telling of things as they truly and really are. If you acknowledge the Word of God, you acknowledge truth in your mind.

Secondly, this is dogmatic realism, for they held to be true what they had been taught. This realism belongs to what has been handed on by the apostolic word spoken and written and accepted with proper apostolic, communal authority rather than from philosophic reflection. A philosopher will not accept anything unless one can assign sufficient reasons for it. The realism that is accepted in God's revealed Word and contained in preaching occurs not from philosophic reflection. One rather attains

---

155 Cf. B.Lonergan 2017, p.223, par.4, p.224, pars.1, 2; also cf. C.O 'O'Donovan, Ibid., p.132

realism through sincere acceptance by a responsible decision to affirm apostolic preaching of what the Word of God revealed.

Thirdly, God's preached Word contains only implicitly this dogmatic realism. We do not say that Isaiah, Paul and others as they preached knew that they were dogmatic realists. We do not say these theologians carried on systematic study and distinguished between the good and the true and between intelligence, deliberation and corresponding truth known by faith affirmation. We affirm, however, that these theologians had intelligence and lived according to the reality they came to know through God's true Word that had been taught by the Apostles.[156].

Though early Christian ante-Nicene authors gave their lives for the faith, they did have a mixture of naïve realism and dogmatic realism in what they said. Believers as they were, they were beyond holding that the only reality was what they could sense and imagine. Above all, they held that what God had revealed to them was real. The dogmatic realist, Lonergan observes, is sure that the real is known through true judgement, but at the same time, the dogmatic realist might be trying to think as well that what he believes could be imagined and could be in space and in time! The one fully naïve realist would say that this tree is real merely because he can see it and touch it.

However, the critical realist would say, yes, one can certainly see the tree and touch it, yet as visible and palpable, it is only sensed (note that one has only been operating on one level of conscious intentionality). For it to be known to be a tree, one needs also to understand what a tree is and then, thirdly, to reach a true judgement to affirm it to exist here in this spot. The

---

156 Cf. O'Donovan, 1976, p.129, par.3; esp. p.137

critical realist might then go on to investigate the matter thoroughly, furnishing sufficient reasons for each of one's assertions.

The dogmatic realist would, as would too the critical realist, rely upon the Word of God, yet the dogmatic realist would not be able to offer so helpful an explanation as to why what one affirms to be so is so. Both dogmatic and critical realists affirm the dogma; however, the dogmatic realist would explain with an admixture of naïve realism; he would hold that those things are distinct where one is not the other, yet he would add that those things that are distinct need to be there in different places and also perhaps that they are there at different times. Practically, the dogmatic realists conceive reality to be spatio-temporal. Again, clearly the effects would depend on causes, but the dogmatic realist needs to see that dependence as, say, brightness emitted by the sun.[157]

6.5 Nicaea, using dogmatic realism, implicitly repudiated naïve realism

6.5a Arius

In a letter to Alexander, Bishop of Alexandria, Arius professed:

> ... the Son ... He (the Father) is his Lord, as being his God and existing before him ...[158] But before he was begotten, before he was created, before he was constituted in being by the Father, he did not exist. For he was not unbegotten.[159]

---

157 Cf. O'Donovan, 1976, pp.132-133

158 Arius' letter to Alexander trans.in O'Donovan, Ibid.p.71, par.1

159 Arius's letter to his fellow student, Eusebius of Nicomedia, trans. In O'Donovan, Ibid. 1976, p.72, par.1

Arius is arguing very clearly and logically, from the terms them-selves: either 'begotten' or 'not begotten', and if 'begotten', then the Son began life being brought into existence and so being created by God. So, the Son is begotten and therefore created by God and unequal with God.

Athanasius did point out that the past participles 'uncreated' (*agenetos*) and 'unbegotten' (*agennetos*) had different meanings and were spelt differently, and yet the Arians were using the terms indiscriminately. Here we notice Arius take leave from the affirmations and dogmas of his religious community in its professions and in its worship. Instead, Arius takes note only of his logical conclusions of sense data. Arius, we find, seems to confine 'generation' to that known by experience and so seems to argue that the Son's generation from the Father has to be within a temporally imagined framework. In this he seems to argue as a naïve realist.

Arius also argues logically and reasonably. He does not seem to be able to grasp and conceive what is strictly immaterial and independent of the spatio-temporal; however, his admixture of naïve realism with rationalism, together with no reliance upon the dogmatic judgement of the believing community, prevents him from accepting the beliefs of the whole religious community. The Bishop of Alexandria reports to bishops on what Arius is saying; namely, that the language that the Arians are using:

> ... runs counter to the meaning of Scripture, (and their language) is
> as follows: for God, who is, brought into existence, out of what was
> non-existent, one who was non-existent ... For the Son is some-
> thing created, something made. He is not similar to the Father in

respect of substance ... The Word is outside of God's substance, other than God's substance, apart from God's substance ...[160]

Arius seemed to hold that one is consubstantial with another because, as he seems to argue from experience, in some measure, even minute, temporally one is derived from the other. At least, Arius might say, the begotten, because he is derived from another – even if not in time – somehow has to come into existence temporally after the one begetting.

I suggest here that Arius does not seem to be able to think, except imaginatively, in order to conceive of a timeless begetting, for he poses as necessary what is in fact a time sequence, though he seems not to be aware of this. Where one begetting has to precede the one begotten in what is nonetheless a temporal sequence, even though he argues he is referring to what is outside time, 'There was when the Son was not.'

As we shall see, Athanasius advances beyond naïve realism to a dogmatic realism. This advance will enable Athanasius to rely first not upon what can be imagined but upon what is truly affirmed in dogmatic beliefs. Athanasius, a dogmatic realist, will say that one is consubstantial with another in that each of them has the same substantial attributes said (understood and truly affirmed) of each.

A realist, as Lonergan understands, relies upon the activity of correct judging to get to truth, and when this judging is operative in attributing and affirming titles to persons, a realist knows by believing that the Father's divinity is in the Son. The critical realist has learnt to identify one's attending to data of sense and of consciousness and to distinguish this attentiveness from

---

160 Alexander of Alexandria reporting on the Arians to the Bishops, 319 A.D., in O'Donovan 1976, p.72, par.4

one's exact, technically understood activities of understanding, conceiving, judging and affirming. The critical realist will distinguish quite radically the act of insight into data from the act of sensing data or of imagining. The critical realist can distinguish insight from intuiting some dispositions in the data for insight. Also, the critical realist will not expect to know what the case is by merely sensing, seeing, hearing, perceiving, imagining, intuiting or conceiving; rather, he or she will affirm one comes to know what is so through correct judgement.

Dogmatic realists could give assent to the truths of faith that have been put to them for acceptance by the religious community. So, dogmatic realists – for example, Tertullian – may confess that Jesus is born eternally of the Father and imagine a moment in eternal time when an event took place where Jesus did emanate from the Father in some imaginable way, but they will not appeal to their imagination as if it was the final authority or benchmark. The dogmatic realists will not ultimately rely upon their ability to imagine in order to decide to affirm if the Father begot the Son eternally. In no way will they follow Arius's example and use their sensing, imagining and reasoning to deny their affirmation of a truth authoritatively handed on to them, for belief, by the believing, worshipping community.

In this case, the dogmatic realist attributes to both Father and Son the titles of each being eternal, without a coming into existence. The dogmatic realist also attributes to the Son that he eternally takes origin in being begotten of the Father, as in the affirmations of the attributes of the *Nicene Creed* recited in Christian churches on Sunday: '... eternally begotten of the Father, God from God, Light from Light, true God from true God; begotten, not made, one in being with the Father. Through Him all things were made ...'.

6.5b Athanasius

Athanasius was a dogmatic realist. He pointed to the titles, 'God', 'the Omnipotent', 'the Lord', 'the Light', 'who takes away sins' being applied in the Scriptures to the Son as well as to the Father. Lonergan observes here that Bishop Alexander of Alexandria preceded Athanasius in noticing that divine titles reserved for the Father were being attributed to the Son as well.

Before the Council of Nicaea, Alexander had taught that 'the Son is less than the Father only in this, that he is not unbegotten'. That is, there was no divine title that the Father enjoyed which the Son did not also have. In using these divine titles of 'Father' and 'Son', in both community prayer and in worship and Scriptures, the community recognized a difference only in that the Son was distinct and was begotten of the Father. Alexander went on to eschew the slightest materialism in the way we were to understand how the Father generated the Son.

Athanasius relied firstly upon the teaching of the believing community. This teaching was evident in the universal affirmations made in the worship of the Church and in the Church's understanding of the Scriptures. Athanasius reports at the Council of Nicaea how the bishops acted as such dogmatic realists:

> But then the bishops, seeing through the deceits of the Arians, went to the Scriptures and there collected these words: 'brightness', 'source', 'stream' and 'the figure of His substance'. They also adduced the phrases: 'in your light we shall see the light' and 'I and the Father are one'. Then, concisely and more clearly,

they wrote that the Son is consubstantial with the Father, for
that is what the other phrases all mean.[161]

Now, Lonergan asks, if we get rid of the least connotation of
materiality from the term 'consubstantial', how can this term
refer to anything? This is a difficulty for the naïve realist who
thinks only of what is real as that which is presented for immediate experience and for inspection by the senses, or by some
idealist peering; however, both the critical realist and the dogmatic realist are able to use this term, 'consubstantial'. Why?
Because for both the critical realist and for the dogmatic realist,
the real is not just something that can be sensed or looked at or
immediately experienced; rather, for them it is through judging
correctly and truly that one gets to know what is real. So, they
can affirm, though they cannot imagine, that the Son has the
same divinity as with the father.[162]

Lonergan also refers to *The Preface for Trinity Sunday,* where it
is said that responding to God's revelation – which in faith we give
assent to about God the Father's glory – that, also without difference or distinction, we hold or judge to be true about His Son and
about His Holy Spirit. And what precisely in faith we give assent
to about the glory of the Father is not that God is some divine
matter; rather, we affirm the truth that has been revealed about
the Father. This truth has been told to us through God's word. So,
then, it is rather that what is true about the Father, we too judge to
be true about the Son and also true about the Holy Spirit, without
any of the Holy Three being said to be less God than the other.[163]

---

161 Athanasius, Letter to the Africans, trans. O'Donovan, 1976, p.99, par.4

162 Cf. O'Donovan, Ibid.1976, p.90, par, 2

163 Cf. O'Donovan, Ibid. 1976. p.90, pars 3-4

We confess that these three are equal in majesty, undivided in splendour, yet one Lord ever to be adored (*The Preface of the Trinity*). That is, we know that each is fully divine with the one same divinity, not because we can imagine this (which we cannot) but because we freely choose to rely upon the most credible witness of all; namely, God's own self-witnessing so we can affirm this divine communion of equals to be true.

Bishop Basil of Caesarea had said that if one wishes to say two are consubstantial, we will have them share the same definition attributed to each. More concretely referring to the Holy Three, Athanasius proposes this understanding by explaining the meaning of 'consubstantial' (*homoousios*) to be (and this is the rule of Athanasius) that what is said of the Father is also to be said of the Son, except that the son is Son and not Father.

Accordingly, too, Athanasius points to these titles – 'God', 'the Omnipotent', 'the Lord', 'the Light', and 'Who takes away our sins' – being used of both Father and Son. These, he says, are applied in the Scripture to the Son as well as to the Father.[164]

In noting the actual development of the notion of consubstantiality, Lonergan's interest is not in the images themselves that were being used in argument – 'offspring from parent, stream from source, brightness from the sun, light from light, fire from fire, or as one torch from another' – but rather in what was grasped in the images; namely, the insight of consubstantiality. It was this idea of consubstantiality, not as it was later, expounded systematically, but as it was grasped then by insight into the then data of sense and of imagination, 'for as in every science, there is an early stage in which insight grasps in data the form or intrinsic intelligibility of

---

164 Cf. O'Donovan, Ibid.1976, p.91, par.3

things, and a later stage in which that insight receives adequate expression'.[165]

We remember how the scientist who was listening to the sermon suddenly grasped a possible solution to a problem vexing him for nigh on two years. How he laboured conceiving and formulating through the afternoon, for he had hurried home to work out more clearly what the idea meant that the insight contained, or rather to conceive or formulate adequately the organization of the data so richly understood and unified by the insight. The scientist did not wish to be distracted by others who might bring up some other image that could remove his attention and focus and occasion him to lose the image or images that were being organized by the insight just caught after waiting so long for it and so lose the actual integration and unity that the insight had gained.

So, Lonergan points out how the Nicene Fathers took the insight into consubstantiality as discovered in those scriptural images and conceived and adapted it as best they could in accord with the Scriptures, in order to conceive that the Father divinely generated his Son,[166] Athanasius, for example, adapted it in this way:

Or who will say that the brightness of the sun is an accident of the sun and not purely and simply the sun's offspring, in such a manner that, while the sun and its brightness are two things, they are nonetheless the one light because the brightness comes from the sun? Since the nature of the Son is even more inseparable from the Father than the brightness of the sun is from the sun itself, and since the divinity of the Son is not something added to him but the divinity of the Father is in the Son, so that

---

165 Cf. O'Donovan, Ibid. 1976, p.97, par.2

166 Cf. O'Donovan, Ibid. 1976, p.100, par.2

whoever sees the son sees the Father in Him, why should the Son who is like this not be called consubstantial with the Father?[167]

We note that Athanasius, in addition to the image of the closest possible union between the sun and its brightness, wants us to go beyond the image and also conceive something unimaginable. Here Athanasius could only put the closest approximation in images to the idea which the insight of consubstantial contained. Lonergan comments:

> Then the final notion of consubstantiality not only transcends every image but also somehow transcends every intelligibility grasped in an image. For just as Maxwell's equation for the electro-magnetic field emerged, in the first place, from images, but have themselves no corresponding image, so the rule of Athanasius refers not to images but only to concepts and to judgements. What the rule states is that what is said of the Father is also to be said of the Son except that the Son is Son and not Father. Not only does this rule prescind from all images; there is nothing imaginable in which it can be grasped or understood.[168]

We grasp then that naïve realism cannot support the dogma of Nicaea. Neither can the council support naïve realism, empiricism, idealism or mere rationalism, for Nicaea's dogma supports the realism of one such as the critical realist and also the dogmatic realist, that relies first upon intelligent inquiry and reasonable affirmation, conceiving and judging in accord with the data of Scripture and teaching tradition of the Church. And such realisms alone can support the Nicene dogma.

---

167 Athanasius writing on the synod trans. O'Donovan, 1976, p.101, par, 1
168 O'Donovan 1976, p.103, par.3.

6.6 The Cappadocians: the known is that affirmed through true judgement. A divine triune life mediated by meaning through conceiving and judging beyond spatio-temporal imagining.

What is the core activity in our knowing? We may be helped to discover this as we read some of the contributions of the Cappadocian Fathers (Bishops Basil of Caesarea, Gregory of Nazianzen and Gregory of Nyssa, in the latter part of the fourth century) as they assimilated the doctrine of consubstantiality of Son with the Father achieved at Nicaea in 325 AD. They relied primarily upon their affirmation of what they came to understand and conceive from the data of their belief and worship. The Cappadocians added their inquiry into the interrelationship between Father and Son and Spirit and how each could be distinguished in the one same, infinite, consubstantial divinity. Gregory of Nazianzen said that each is fully God and none is more divine than another, nor does any exercise the divine willing without the other two acting as one with Him. Indeed, the three persons act like three suns adjoined that produce the one light.[169]

Gregory of Nyssa adds that in the exercise of this common, divine, saving action towards us, all creative activity of God '... originates from the Father, proceeds through the Son and is brought to fulfilment in the Holy Spirit'.[170]

The Cappadocians made great advances in speaking of the distinction among the consubstantial three. What has the Father that the others do not have? 'Fatherhood,' Basil answered. The Son? 'Sonship,' he added. The Spirit? Here, the two Gregorys would add

---

169 Gregory of Nazianzen, The Trinity, trans. Bettenson, 1974, p.115, par.2

170 Cf. Gregory of Nyssa, The Trinity, trans Bettenson 1974, p.153, par. 3

clearly that what the Spirit has to distinguish Him in this immanent relating among the three consubstantial persons was 'procession'. So, the Cappadocians brought into theology the claim that the three consubstantial divine persons were distinguished among themselves, one from the other, by mutual relationships of origin.

Gregory of Nyssa explains that while we accept that the divine nature is perfectly the same, we at the same time affirm that which causes is distinct from that which is caused. For, Nyssa continues, one is derived immediately from the first cause, another through the one that is immediately derived. So, it is precisely through causing in divinity that one can distinguish one person from another. Again, the one that causes another first and immediately causes a second one mediately through the one immediately caused. So, Nyssa notes the one caused immediately is distinct from the one mediately caused.

The Son is clearly the only-begotten but does not exclude the Spirit who, through the Son mediating, is able to relate to the Father by way of nature. Also, Nyssa emphasizes that while one speaks of divinity containing a causing and a caused, this causing does not denote a diversity of nature[171], but only a difference in manner of existence.[172]

These Cappadocian bishops were speaking of how each divine person was unique and distinct yet each having the one same divinity. The Cappadocians named their uniqueness and distinctness arising because of their mutual divine, eternal, immanent relationships of origin in the one same divinity. They were not speaking of any temporal relating to us, any dealing with us in a certain time, that caused in them their eternal distinction! This would make God temporally dependent on a

---

171 Gregory of Nyssa, The Trinity, trans. by Bettenson, 1974, p. 154, par 3.

172 Gregory of Nyssa, Ibid. pp.154-5

creature for God's own inner divine, triune life! And such a conclusion the Cappadocians, who were focusing on the meaning of consubstantiality and the Holy Divine Three, would abhor.

For Nyssa said, one thinks of the unbegotten Father, and straightway we think of the Son with him, 'without any interval of separation; and through the Son and with the Son, in inseparable conjunction, the Holy Spirit is thought of as existing without the interposition of any idea of an empty and insubstantial gap...' Nyssa goes on to say that the Spirit comes through the Son from the Father yet 'not being divided from the Father and the Son either by temporal interval or by diversity of nature. There are no intervals in their sphere of existence.'[173]

6.7 The naïve realist 'fancies he knows it (the world mediated by meaning) by taking a good look at what is going on out there now'. How does the naïve realist seek to know God?

We find that the object in the world of immediacy, as Lonergan says, is already, out there now, real. In the world of immediacy, all it takes to be objective is to be 'a successfully functioning animal'.[174] We can say the piece of cheese on the bench is an object for the mouse, and the mouse behind the hole in the wall is an object to the cat waiting outside, slowly wagging its tail.

However, in the world of meaning, to be objective is a more demanding thing than to be objective in the world of immediacy where one just has to use one's senses and be a successively functioning animal. Lonergan defines the object in the world mediated

---

173 Gregory of Nyssa, Ibid. p.157, par, 2; p.158, par.1

174 Gregory of Nyssa, Ibid., p.263, par.3; B.Lonergan, 1992, pp.276-277.

by meaning: 'It is what is intended by the question, and it is what becomes understood, affirmed, decided by the answer'.[175] Indeed, 'Being, for me, is the universe, the world mediated by meaning. It's the answer to what you know when you answer questions that regard everything about everything'.[176] It definitely is not solely the world of animal sensing, the 'taken-for-granted' or the world of the 'already-out-there-now-real'. Once one gets a rather startling grasp how one has been acting upon such a naïve realist conviction, and understands from then on that, rather, the real is the verified, one is being intellectually converted.

Let us revise what we mean in regard to our questions – as Lonergan says, putting us into immediate relationship with objects in the world mediated by meaning – and our answers relating us mediately to the same objects. Indeed, we only relate to objects inasmuch as they are answers to questions. To be objective in the world mediated by meaning first implies that one is experiencing data being given through sensing and through being conscious. Secondly, it implies carrying out those activities that bring one to be intelligent and reasonable; that is, grasping insight, formulating, weighing evidence and verifying. So, one needs not only to be experiencing one's action and oneself acting but one is also consciously focused upon carrying out the normative activities required to be intelligent and reasonable. Thirdly, to be objective in the world mediated by meaning,

---

175 B.Lonergan, , 2017, p, 246 , par.3; also note, "God certainly is not an object in the naïve realist sense.." nor "an object if one retreats from naïve realism to an empiricism, a naturalism, a positivism, or an idealism. But if by an object one means anything that is intended in questions and known through correct answers, anything within the world mediated by meaning, then ...." 2017, p.316, par.2ff

176 B.Lonergan, 2016, An interview with Fr.B.Lonergan"p.184, pars 4, 5

one has to persist in the normative activities just mentioned and
reach the ultimate, absolute moment of a reflective act of understanding that proceeds exigently to judgement and affirmation.

> This larger world, mediated by meaning, does not lie within
> anyone's immediate experience. It is not even the sum, the
> integral, of the totality of all worlds of immediate experience.
> For meaning is an act that does not merely repeat but goes
> beyond experiencing. For what is meant is what is intended
> in questioning and is determined not only by experience but
> also by understanding and commonly, by judgement as well'[177]

This final moment is an absolute one, for this activity of reflective
insight and proceeding to give assent in judgement are the absolute components in being objective. This judging sublates and
completes the prior two components in being objective; namely,
the experiencing of pertinent data and the carrying out of what is
normative questioning and answering or, in other words, being
intelligent and reasonable in regards to that data experienced.
It is absolute in that, through judging, one transcends what one
senses and imagines, understands and formulates and feels, to
arrive at what is in fact so and true. One gets beyond one's subjective activity, whatever one's feeling or doing may be, or whatever
the activity of others may be and accomplish. What is arrived
at is being.

That Caesar crossed the Rubicon is a fact – it is true, it is the
case. It enjoys the absoluteness of what is, so that in the world
mediated by meaning, the object known is what is, and it is that

---

177 B.Lonergan, 2017, p, 75, par.2; also, "This addition of understanding
       and judgment is what makes possible the world mediated by meaning,
       ..." Lonergan, Ibid.

which is intelligently grasped and reasonably affirmed in the data of experience. And what is verified enjoys absolute objectivity. What is true is permanent; the meaning something possessed in its own context can never be denied truthfully.[178]

All this is in sharp contrast to the world of the taken-for-granted, the world of the 'already-out-there-now-real', for Lonergan reminds us that in the taken-for-granted world, where one is no longer in the world mediated by meaning, one is back in the world of immediacy. Here, one engages in picture-thinking, and here an object is something that one needs to be able to look at. Accordingly, knowing has to be something like looking, peering, seeing, intuiting, perceiving. And again, for one to be objective in the world of immediacy, it suffices to take a good, long, hard look to see all that is there to be seen. And the object known is something that one looks at.

For the critical realist, however, in the world of immediacy there is but the givenness of an object, but givenness is mere data as yet unknown. Only by adding understanding and judging (the normative and absolute components of objectivity) can one get to knowing, and so one does not do this by some sort of mere looking, sensing, perceiving or intellectual peering.[179] One has to learn to identify for oneself one's own interior cognitional activities of each of the four levels of intentional consciousness in self-transcendence in order to find out for oneself what knowing

---

178 "what God has revealed and the church has infallibly declared, is true. What is true is permanent: the meaning it possessed in its own context can never be denied truthfully." Lonergan, 2017, p.301, par.1; cf.ibid.p.300

179 Cf. B.Lonergan, 2017, "two quite disparate meanings of the term, object..." 246, par.3, cf.also par.5, pp.247-8.

is.[180] Then one is in a position to be a critical realist. One is then, Lonergan says, able to grasp intelligently, and reasonably to affirm, in the data of one's own cognitional experience when one is knowing and when one is not.

One can know what is real, for experiencing data of sense and of consciousness is but operating on the first level of intentional consciousness, to provide data for understanding and then for judging:

> The mere givenness of inner or outer actuality ... truly is no more
> than the condition for the rational transition from the affirmation
> of possible to the affirmation of actual contingent being.[181]

6.8 An analogy to gain a minimal understanding of how three distinct persons are in the one unlimited, intelligent being

What was noted from the very first chapter in this book was the reflective insight in Chief Inspector Hubbard that occurred on Mr Wendice opening the door with the missing key. Instantly the Inspector, in that reflective understanding, was conscious that in answering the final relevant question, he had met all the requirements to proceed to judgement. Indeed, he was

---

180 Cf. B.Lonergan, 2017, p.18, par.2; also cf. Ibid. pp.18-19; one must distinguish the normative pattern immanent in our conscious and intentional operations and objectifications of that pattern . These objectifications cannot change but only arrive at a more adequate account of the dynamic structure of human consciousness, that does not admit revision. In fact one would have to use this pattern to carry out any revision of it. Cf. B.Lonergan, 2017,p.21,pars. 3-4; p.22, pars.1-3; also, Lonergan, 1988, pp.209-211.

181 B.Lonergan, 1997, p.99, par.1

simultaneously conscious that he not only had sufficient reason to proceed to judgement but that he was conscious he was being rationally driven to proceed to give assent and to judge that Mr Wendice was guilty and Mrs Wendice innocent. Further, with giving assent to the value of her innocence, he was instantly now, whereas he had not been before, conscious of being driven responsibly to decide to have her set free.

In the actual happening, he is conscious then of two processions or of two emanations. The first emanation he is conscious of is that he has to be rational and to proceed to judge as reason demands: Wendice is guilty, Mrs Wendice is innocent. This emanation calls forth a second emanation in which he is conscious of being driven to be responsible and to decide to set Mrs Wendice free.

So, Inspector Hubbard was conscious of there occurring these two emanations or processions. Importantly, both were intelligently linked. That is, because of his reflective insight, he had to proceed on to judging her innocent, and because of his being able now to affirm her innocence, he had to proceed responsibly to have her set free. So, in his own very consciousness, the three activities; namely, his reflective insight, his judging and his deciding, were distinct but totally interrelating, correlative and interdependent. His three activities were linked through his being conscious of the same reflective understanding, intelligently supporting each activity with warranty to proceed intelligently, rationally and responsibly.

These three distinct, conscious activities – reflective understanding, assenting, and deciding to love – offer a comparison for the Trinity. We can clearly identify three distinct divine, conscious activities. The one divinity is conscious and fully intelligent from infinite, reflective grasp of all the evidence that there ought be divine loving. This divine conscious understanding is a subsistent activity and so is conscious and personal. This conscious subsistent proceeds intelligently to affirm this insight. The judgement itself is subsistent activity and so personal, and conscious of the infinite reasonableness for the expression of the value grasped; and this infinitely correct judgement, or inner word, is living and conjoined to and a perfect likeness of the one subsistent insight originating it. So, this 'generation' we term 'Father and Son'. Also, they are fully intelligent and aware they are divinely responsible that their divine correct judgement must originate a corresponding decision to love.

This decision is subsistent, and so personal – the Spirit. It is also conscious and intelligent of proceeding *because of* the Father grasping its eternal value that there ought be divine love and *because of* the Son's affirming that same value. The Spirit, because of being intelligent of this same understanding and judging that are Father and Son, consciously emanates responsibly in love in accord with the Father's and the Son's spiration of that love through their understanding and judging. That is, the Spirit is proceeding responsible love, fully conscious and intelligent of originating from both Father and Son.

> The Holy Spirit also is one, and we proclaim him singly, attached to the one Father through the one Son, through himself completing the worshipful and blessed Trinity.[182]

Lonergan makes an original contribution by noting and properly assessing that the divine consciousness is obtaining throughout in the divine processions.[183] In the one same infinite, divine

---

182 Basil of Caesarea, The Trinity, trans. Bettenson, 1974, p.76, par.2

183 'Either consciousness is brought in all along the line or it is not brought in at all. Starting from an account of the psychological analogy that

consciousness, two emanations bring forth mutual relationships of origin in the one divinity. So, in regard to the first divine procession, Lonergan says:

> ... the divine reflective understanding grasps ... that infinite perfection is love, rational love. This necessitates the judgement: there must be love. This judgement occurs within the consciousness of the infinite act. Because it occurs within God, it must be infinite.[184]

> We all know by experience how a rash judgement differs from a true judgement ... The former is elicited without sufficient reason. The true judgement, however, is based on the evidence itself grasped within a certain intellectual necessity that does not allow a true judgement to be avoided. For what was wanting in rash judgement and is found in true judgement is called an intellectual or intelligible emanation. And this very emanation is nothing else than this: that whoever grasps sufficient evidence, in the very act of grasping this sufficiency, brings forth a true judgement through a sort of necessity that is intellectually conscious.[185]

The second procession is responsibly to originate as proceeding divine love. The Father and Son originate divine love because

---

is strictly psychological, we have processions that pertain to the field of consciousness, relations that pertain to the field of consciousness, subsistent relations will be conscious subjects...the whole treatise on the trinity ... integration all along the line is had when the psychological analogy is taken in a genuinely psychological sense" B.Lonergan, 1996 (CWL 6) " Consciousness and the Trinity", p.127, par.1.

184 B.Lonergan, 1996, p.140, par.2

185 B.Lonergan , 1959, p.57, par.4, trans. Peter Beer.

of their being conscious of an infinite demand to be responsible
and so to act in rational accord with the divine judgement that
it is divinely worthwhile for them to originate divine love:

> We all know from experience the difference between an inordi-
> nate act of the will that is repugnant to reason and an ordered
> act of the will that is authentic, binding and holy. For the good-
> ness grasped by insight and approved by reason and imposed
> on the will so obliges us that we either, as irrational people,
> choose what is contrary to right reason, or else, as rational
> people, accede to what the intellect demands ...
>
> What is lacking in a morally bad act is however present in
> a morally good act, namely that spiritual and moral procession,
> which so effectively binds the will that not only ought we love
> what is good but also actually do love it. This procession is also
> a certain intellectual or intelligible emanation, since it consists
> in this that, because of the good being understood, the appe-
> tite that is potentially reasonable becomes actually reasonable.
> Because of this, since by nature the will is a rational appetite,
> and as this appetite cannot be actually rational unless it actu-
> ally follows reason, it has necessarily been said that 'love cannot
> proceed except by following a concept of the intellect'.[186]

Again, the Father understands assent has to proceed because of it
being fully rational that there be divine love. So, the Father proceeds to bring forth conscious divine assenting, the Son. Also, the
Father and the Son understanding and assenting consciously to
the value of there being divine love, are both conscious of their
consequent divine responsibility that there originate divine loving.

---

186 B.Lonergan, Ibid. p.58, par.2

There are then two processions that may be conceived in God. They are not unconscious processes but intellectually, rationally, morally conscious as are judgements of value based on the evidence perceived by a lover, and the acts of loving grounded on judgements of value.[187]

So we arrive at an analogy, having refined out all created limitations and dependence, all temporal and spatial succession and entitative separation and dependence. There obtains only distinct (not imaginatively separate), intelligible correlations because of intellectual emanations of origin. Only present is pure perfection of intellectual (intelligent and intelligible) and rational and responsible emanations.

> ... the Father is God in a manner analogous to the grasp of sufficient evidence that necessitates one to judge; the Son is God in the same consciousness but now a consciousness analogous to that of the dependence of the judgement on the grasp of sufficient evidence; the Holy Spirit is the same consciousness in a third manner; namely, as the dependence of the act of love on the grasp of sufficient evidence and the rational affirmation.[188]

---

187 B.Lonergan, 2017 "A Third Collection" p.91, par.5

188 Also note "The same consciousness is had differently by three persons" B.Lonergan, 1996,(CWL 6) p.135, par.3

Chapter 7

In inquiry there are eight functional specialties in the process from data to results: a single process that 'can be adapted to any subject in which investigations were responding to past history and were to influence future history'. [189]

---

189 Cf. B.Lonergan, 2017, p.130, par.5; cf. ch.5; cf.B.Lonergan, 1984, 488, par.2

Conversion
Subject in self-giving love
transforms one's world

Deciding
4: <u>Level D</u> *Dialectic* →
to manifest decisions,
opposed stances in their
roots; how they came to
disagree.

5: D *Foundations* →
to explain newly chosen
direction set by conversions
intellectual, moral, religious;
sets framework for 6, 7, 8.

Judging
3: <u>Level J</u> *History special
aim* → to judge what was
going forward culturally,
doctrinally, institutionally;
General aim: to know how all
movements are interacting,
conspiring.

6: J *Doctrines* →
to judge fact, value in
convert's new living:
doctrines in variety, function,
variation, development,
permanence, cultural
pluralism and unity of faith.

Understanding
2: <u>Level U</u> *Interpretation* →
to understand what was
meant. Grasp context,
horizons, interests.

7: U *Systematics* →
to gain some understanding
of affirmed values, facts
values, spiritual things, in
appropriate systems of
conceptualization.

Experience
1: <u>Level E</u> *Research* →
to provide data relevant
to inquiry: In general – fills
museums, dictionaries.
Special – for special question.

8: E *Communications* →
to present understanding
from systematics to hearts
and minds of all peoples,
cultures.

In reference to the above diagram:

- Note two phases of investigative operations: (1) to listen, receive (research, interpretation, history,

dialectic) and (2) to bear witness (foundations, doctrines, systematics, communications).

- Our conscious intentional activities occur on four distinct
levels; namely, of experiencing, understanding, judging
and deciding. Each level has it own proper goal.

- Scientifically, the goal proper to any level may be the
objective sought by operations on all four levels.[190]

- Phase 1: inquiry moves from data, through meanings
and facts to personal encounter. Phase 2 begins from
reflecting on authentic conversion, which is used as a
horizon within which one grasps what doctrines mean,
and grasps minimal yet fruitful understanding offered
in doctrines, to come finally to explore cultural com-
munication through media.

- Lonergan's contribution: to conceive these specialities as distinct stages in a single process from data to
ultimate results.[191]

- Specialities interdependent, reciprocal dependence
within Phases 1 and 2.[192]

7.1 Can we get some understanding of how transcendental method achieves an organization and integration of specialist tasks operating in the process from inquiry into data on to the achievement of ultimate results?

7.1a First specialty task: research

As Inspector Hubbard entered the apartment of Mr and Mrs
Wendice, his police staff were gathering any piece of material

---

190 CCf. B.Lonergan, 2017, p.127, par.7; p.128

191 Cf. B.Lonergan. 2017, p.130, par.5

192 Cf. B.Lonergan, 2017, p.134, pars.5, 6; p.135, pars.4, 5; p.136, pars.1-3.

that could be connected with what had happened. They had not moved the body and the scissors were still embedded in the back of the body of the man on the floor. The scissors themselves would hopefully have valuable fingerprints on them. The husband, as he put the tray of teacups on the writing desk, deliberately moved the blotting pad to let there be uncovered a stocking hidden beneath. The police had already discovered a letter in the pocket of the dead man. The dead man on the floor had no personal identification on him.

The Inspector was anxious to meet any person who could provide information on what had happened. Straightaway he met Mrs Wendice and Mr Wendice introduced himself. So, pertinent people, as yet providing merely their names, were available. Possible relevant pieces of material as to who, when and where, persons of interest were being assembled for questioning by the Inspector as to their possible involvement in *how* or *why* the killing had happened. Already, items and people connected to the killed man were now available as a result of the police search.

The Inspector, on questioning Mrs Wendice, also began to grasp an understanding of *what* had happened. She had manifested how she had been in bed and had got up to answer the phone. From where she had stood, behind the desk, an assassin had stepped out from behind her and tried to strangle her with a scarf. The Inspector asked if a scarf had been found. The police had not seen the husband burn the scarf. Instead, we had seen a stocking hidden by the husband so that the police, on finding it, could lead them to think that Mrs Wendice was manufacturing evidence, for the marks on her throat were not those made by a stocking. But a scarf, that she claimed to have been tied around her neck, could not be found.

Data for questioning: research.

7.1b Second specialty task: interpretation, understanding of data collected

The second task is in regards to the killing of a Mr Swan. The Inspector, by putting various observations together and discovering that Mrs Wendice had been lying to him, began to get an idea that she was covering up a lot more. Indeed he began to be highly suspicious of her whole story. Also, upon the love letter from Mr Halliday to Mrs Wendice being discovered in the pocket of the dead man, it could seem she had killed him in order to gain this letter of hers that had been stolen by her husband, unbeknownst to her. She had lost the sympathy of the jury by her affair with Mr Halliday.

So, from the examination of relevant pieces of material found and from questioning what they had meant, the Inspector had succeeded to come up with a possible explanation of why the dead man was killed. Mrs Wendice would have benefited by the removal from the scene of the man dead on the floor.

Interpretation!

7.1c Third specialty task: history

Which understanding or interpretation of the whole course of events in the killing of a Mr Swan could be believed? There were all the pieces of relevant material found, all that Mrs Wendice, Mr Wendice and Mr Halliday had to say in witness. Indeed, things began to point in the direction for a theory to be made that Mrs Wendice had conspired to murder her blackmailer. All had to be questioned. All evidence had to be weighed for and against the theory of her guilt. In fact, according to the evidences brought forward at the trial, the jury found themselves satisfied that enough doubt had been removed for them to give a reasonable judgment in verdict, accepting as true the conspiracy theory of how Mrs Wendice had lured her blackmailer to his death.

The jury brought in a verdict of guilty. The jury were now considering all the activity of researching and interpreting or understanding carried out by all the police and detectives helping Chief Inspector Hubbard. These had shared in the research of pertinent data and they had shared their understandings of the various sets of data with the Chief Inspector. The Chief Inspector had reported his findings to the Crown Advocate who had presumably fashioned, together with the Chief Inspector, the hypothesis of Mrs Wendice's guilt.

In the Old Bailey courtroom, the research police and Inspectors gave their registering of data and also their opinions under the direction of the attorney/barrister prosecuting for the Crown who was proposing the theory or advocating that Mrs Wendice was guilty.

When both sides of the case had presented witnesses, and the lawyers had questioned these witnesses for and against the accused, it was presumed that no further relevant data or questions could be presented. Experiential objectivity had been operating in the work of assembling relevant data and the evidence of relevant witnesses.

The barristers then proposed possible opposing opinions (second level of intentional consciousness) and had begun to weigh evidence for and against the case for prosecution (third level of intentional consciousness). This weighing of evidence continued in the jury room. The jurors persisted in raising and answering relevant questions considered in the courtroom in order that they find an answer to the final relevant question (normative objectivity).When they did grasp this final answer, they understood that they in fact had reached an unconditioned verdict where they had met all conditions needed in allowing them to make their judgment in verdict beyond reasonable doubt (absolute objectivity).

They would report to the Judge that they had found they understood no further relevant question remained to be answered and that it was beyond reasonable doubt that the accused was guilty.

The judge whose office it was to accept the finding of the jury and so to concur with their judgment, if in his judgement all had proceeded in due order, would also hand down sentence with his judgment. The Judge was adjoining his authoritative judging to the judging of the jury. The Judge's verdict was the legitimate and historical outcome of her public trial. This judgment gave as fact her guilt in the murder of Mr Swan. That was the historical judgment recorded at her trial and it sublated all the movement of all the research, investigation of opinions and debate at the trial and in the jury room.

History!

7.1d   Fourth specialty task: dialectic

This clearly presents the different stances of those taking part in this trial. The opposing attorneys or barristers took up differing stances and viewpoints. They mustered their witnesses to support their line of argument. They did not inquire into evidence to provide support to the argument of the opposing side. It is not that they were biased but that they devoted the time available to acquiring full enough evidence to support their own stances.

The jury had a higher office to perform. The jury had to weigh the most telling arguments of each side, had to proceed from moral conversion and be alert to the presence of bias, or to lack of attentiveness, a lack of understanding and indeed a lack of correct understanding in the arguments presented in the courtroom. The jury had to proceed till all the relevant questions had been raised and answered in order that the truth might appear.

Coming to a reflective insight by means of a detached and disinterested inquiry, free from bias, and finding this correctness stood up to persistent questioning, they were to bring in their finding to the Judge and court. The jury had to act by a dialectic informed with intellectual and moral conviction.

The Judge then took a stand that sublated all the judgments in court. He lived to serve the law. He had seen to proper procedure during the trial. The Judge was requiring proper procedure to obtain, in the presentation of evidence, that no relevant data would be prevented from being presented at the trial. He was not to argue so one-sidedly as had the two opposing attorneys in front of him. He was to act as judge and custodian of proper legal procedure throughout the trial. He honestly sought that the truth might appear without bias or favour. So, he accepted the jury's finding.

The judge acting according to his duty as judge of the realm and passed sentence according to the deed as required by the law. He acted intelligently and reasonably. He took his stand by the proper procedure of the law of the land in regards to the verdict brought in by the jury. On that process, he took his stand. It was a different stance from that of the Defence Attorney and of the Prosecution Attorney, who both took differing and opposed stances to one another.

Conversion: intellectual conversion at least in that for judge and court, it be held that the true was the verified, and truth was not merely what a person imagined, saw, or was by feeling partial to. Instead, what people said had to be questioned and reasons for and against had to be weighed in regards to any theory formulated by the attorneys for either side in the trial. The Judge had to wait until the final relevant questions had been raised and answered. The Judge was to be a man of intellectually open mind. He was thus ever open to a true possibility of inquiry, even unfinished inquiry where this was permitted by law. He was devoted to the truth to be found, not by mere experiencing or looking but by persistent questioning. The Judge (as would a morally converted person) had to be devoted to what was right and good and would not permit biases to interfere with the due process of law in his courtroom.

7.1e   Fifth specialty task: foundations

There was some commitment to intellectual and moral conversion evident on the part of those taking part in the trial. Such commitment was evident in the Judge as he presided over the due process of law being carried out in his courtroom. He was open to there being heard pertinent evidence at the trial and was open to the weighing up of that evidence in having heard the arguments for and against the conviction of the accused. He was also open to further admittance of unheard, relevant evidence. He was convinced that the truth was not merely to be had on what appeared to be the case but that truth was to be found if all relevant questions had in fact been raised and answered, so that the truth was that which was intelligently grasped and reasonably affirmed in the complete relevant data. He manifested this standpoint proper to that of a critical realist stance. Such was his wont and conviction.

7.1f   Sixth specialty task: doctrines

The Judge espoused the legitimate laws of the country. He proceeded according to law in receiving the verdict duly processed, and he passed judgment according to the law. The Judge and the Inspector held that justice must be done. For this, all relevant questions had to be raised and answered. Truth and justice had to be served.

Both the Judge and the Inspector could well set out these convictions in suitable expressions. So, upon request by the Home Secretary who had been duly informed by Chief Inspector Hubbard, and because of the recently uncovered evidence, the Judge grasped the genuine, undeniable possibility that the husband could well have conspired to have his wife murdered. Accordingly, the Judge allowed the testing of the new hypothesis that might well allow for the case to be reopened. This conviction of being open to relevant questions being heard and answered we may presume was paramount in the Judge's life and suitably expressed in the Judge's rulings.

7.1g   Seventh specialty task: systematic investigation

Inspector Hubbard proceeded to carry out his two experiments that embodied the two final relevant questions to be raised and answered in proper, rational order.

Firstly, the Inspector arranged the experiment where what rationally was the penultimate question could be raised and answered as to whether or not Mrs Wendice knew of the key being under the carpet. Only then could the ultimate relevant question be raised and answered.

The final relevant question was answered as Wendice opened the door of the apartment with his wife's missing key.

This event allowed for the reflective understanding that warranted the Inspector to readily give assent to Mr Wendice being the guilty party. Those in court later – the Judge and jury – could rely upon the credible witness of Chief Inspector Hubbard and proceed to pass verdict of known guilt upon the husband. So, this further understanding of the case proceeded as a result of the final relevant questions and answers being put in order in this systematic way and manifested to the court.

Bias was carefully guarded against and eschewed. Formal steps of well-practised investigation, though formulated in legal terms that in part could be incipiently systematic terms for legal procedures, were observed. At any rate, the answers won gave a complete wholeness of understanding and explanation to the investigation of the whole case.

Here we see a crossing over again to the tasks in the first phase, where the judgement of history is improved upon in light of the truth won by the later systematic inquiry. This truth resulted from relevant answers and understanding gained from uncovering new answers to new final but most relevant questions. Here, then, the later systematic investigation influenced the third task of history in the case.

7.1h Eighth specialty task: communications!

Finally, this happy result for the triumph of justice and openness to truth and a full, satisfactory explanation would have been published and handed down by the Judge and then published in the newspapers for all the people to rejoice in.

7.2 Diagram: eight functional specialties in proceeding for any topic from data to ultimate results

Conversion
Intellectually, morally, religiously

4: D I choose this
judgement
Level of decision ➔
where I stand

5: D I choose this
direction in life
Level of decision
for 6, 7, 8

3: J I judge this to have
been going forward
Level of judging

6: J I judge true this
value proposed
Level of judging

2: U I understand what
was meant
Level of
understanding

7: U I understand how
facts, values fit
together.
I grasp whole course of
events and meanings
Level of understanding

1: E I provide data
relevant to inquiry
Level of experiencing

8: E I share with others
understanding
won by systematics
organising
Level of experiencing
Data for
communications

7.3   Lonergan's contribution: to conceive these eight specialties as distinct stages in a single process from data to ultimate results

Our two phases in functional specialties, Lonergan says, correspond with this division: if one encounters the past, one also has to take one's stand towards the future. Indeed, these eight functional specialties 'can be adapted to any subject in which investigations were responding to past history and were to influence future history'.[193]

Accordingly, let us take literature studies. One will study in two phases. Firstly, we listen to what Shakespeare achieved in his poetry and plays, and we also read what Donne and so-called metaphysical poets left us and what, later, English schools of literature presented. We inquire as to what it all meant for literature then. We take those periods in English literature when the language really ticked over and concentrate our inquiry on them (FR Leavis in his little book, *Education and the university*, tells how he came to discover this wisdom of not trying to cover everything in ascertaining what the past had to teach the students at Downing College, Cambridge). We first take in the past in order that we ascertain what helpful influence can be gauged for literary critical studies today. In both first and second phases of this method, we use the transcendental method of the transcendental precepts, the threefold conversions and triple cord of objectivity and worlds of meaning. So, we can find what was of value in literary criticism in such past literature, and secondly, so we can be able to share with others the meaning and value we have won from our study.

Each level of conscious and intentional operations has its own

---

193 B.Lonergan, 1984, p. 488, par.2; cf. B.Lonergan, 2017, p.130, par.5. cf. Lonergan 2017, p129, pars.2-4.; p.130, pars.2 & 3

aim to achieve: provision of data, insight, judgement, decision. But everyday commonsense knowing does not distinguish the four levels of conscious intentionality. Instead, in commonsense knowing, all four levels are being used without being distinguished so that no functional specialization arises. It is then that no particular goal of any of the four level activities is aimed at. The commonsense goal here then is that which results not from any particular level but is that which comes from all the levels cumulatively working altogether. In scientific inquiry, operations of all four levels may take as object the goal aimed at by one particular level. In the specialty task of research:

> ... the textual critic will select (fourth level of decision) the method he believes will enable him to discover (level of understanding) that which one may reasonably affirm (level of judgement) was written in the original text (level of experience). So, the textual critic is working on all four levels, but his goal is the end proper to the first level; namely, to ascertain the data. The interpreter, however, pursues a different goal ... [194]

That is, one working in any specialty task needs to be operating out of all four levels of conscious intentionality in order to achieve the goal of that level; say, of assembling data for research (making intelligible the Rosetta Stone), for the textual critic may not just work on the levels of understanding and of selective decision, the second and fourth levels. The textual critic has to work on the first level in order to apprehend the text accurately before he can possibly understand it. And then too he has to judge his understanding to be correct (third intentional level

---

194 B.Lonergan, 2017, p.128, par.3

activity); otherwise he will fail to distinguish between understanding and misunderstanding.

As one reflects on the table of specialist tasks in any topic
of investigation, in the first phase (tasks 1 to 4), one first ascer-
tains data (task 1) and moves up through the meanings (task2)
and facts gained (task3) to personal encounter (task 4). Then,
in the second phase of investigation, beginning by reflecting on
authentic conversion (genuine openness and commitment to the
transcendental precepts) and threefold conversion (intellectual,
moral and religious), one uses conversion as the horizon (task 5)
within which to apprehend stances and policies (task 6) and to
understand them (task 7), and finally to discover how to com-
municate this meaning (task 8).[195]

7.4   Why eight specialties?

Lonergan here has brought in something new in that he conceives of these distinct levels and parts of inquiry as functional
specialties, or tasks, as distinct and separable stages in a single
process from data to ultimate results.[196] It is important to note
that functional specialization is not a distinction of specialists
but a distinction of specialties. It is also important to distinguish
different tasks. In each of the two phases, the four ends correspond to the four levels of conscious and intentional operations.
This differentiation aids one to grasp the distinct scientific tasks
to be focused upon. They are tasks that enable one to move from
data to ultimate results in one's field of inquiry.

---

195 Cf. B.Lonergan, 2017, p.130, pars.2&.3

196 B.Lonergan, 2017, p.130, par.5

Conversion

Dialectic ➔ stand taken Foundations ➔ convictions

History ➔ judgement   Doctrines ➔ positions

Interpretation ➔ theories Systematics ➔ explanation

Research ➔ data   Communications ➔ publicity

These eight ends exist. So, then, there are eight different tasks to be performed, and each of the eight tasks has its proper excellence. None can stand without the other seven. All of the eight tasks are needed for the complete process from data to results in any inquiry that responds to the past and which is to influence the future.[197]

---

197 Cf.B.Lonergan, 2017,p.130, pars.4-6; p.131.pars. 1-4

Works consulted

1959

B Lonergan, *Divinarum personarum conceptionem analogicam*, 2nd ed., Gregorian University Press, Rome, 1959.

1964

B Lonergan, *De Deo Trino VI*, 3rd ed., Gregorian University Press, Rome, 1964. (Collected works of Bernard Lonergan, vols 11–12, University of Toronto Press for the Lonergan Research Institute of Regis College, Toronto, hereafter CWL 11–12.)

1972

B Lonergan, *Method in theology*, Darton, Longman & Todd, London, 1972, (CWL 14).

1974

B Lonergan, *A second collection: papers by Bernard JF Lonergan SJ*, eds William FJ Ryan and Bernard J Tyrell, Darton, Longman & Todd, London, 1974, (CWL 13).

1976

Cornelius O'Donovan, *The way to Nicea*, Darton, Longman & Todd, London, 1976.

1984

B Lonergan, *Method of theology institute (unpublished)*, Lonergan Research Institute, Regis College, Toronto, 1984.

1985

B Lonergan, *A third collection: papers by Bernard JF Lonergan SJ*, eds Frederick E Crowe, Paulist, New York, 1985, (CWL 16).

1988

B Lonergan, *Collection*, 2nd ed., eds Frederick E Crowe and Robert M Doran, University of Toronto Press, Toronto, 1988, (CWL 4).

1990

B Lonergan, *Understanding and being*, eds Elizabeth A Morelli and Mark D Morelli, revised and augmented by Frederick E Crowe with the collaboration of Elizabeth Morelli, Mark Morelli, Robert M Doran and Thomas V Daly, University of Toronto Press, Toronto, 1990, (CWL 5).

1992

B Lonergan, *Insight: a study of human understanding*, 5th ed., (1957), first revised and augmented by Frederick E Crowe and Robert M Doran, University of Toronto Press, Toronto, 1992, (CWL 3).

1996

B Lonergan, *Consciousness and the trinity*, Philosophical and theological papers, 2nd ed., North American College, Rome, lecture (January 1963), 1996, (CWL 6).

1997

B Lonergan, *Verbum: word and idea in Aquinas*, (1st ed., David Burrell, 1967), revised and augmented by Frederick E Crowe and Robert M Doran, University of Toronto Press, Toronto, 1997, (CWL 2).

2004
B Lonergan, *Philosophical and theological papers*, eds Robert C Croken and Robert M Doran, (CWL 17).

2016
B.Lonergan, *A Second Collection*,2nd Edit. Eds. Robert M Doran and John D Dadosky, Lonergan Research Institute , Regis College, University of Toronto Press(CWL 13)

2017
B.Lonergan, *Method in Theology*, 2nd Edit. Eds. Robert M Doran and John D Dadosky, Lonergan Research Institute , Regis College, University of Toronto Press(CWL 14)

2017
B.Lonergan, *A Third Collection* , 2nd Edit.,Eds. Robert M Doran and John D Dadosky, Lonergan Research Institute , Regis College, University of Toronto Press(CWL 16)

Gratitude is expressed to the editors of *The collected works of Bernard Lonergan* for permission for references from these volumes.

Gratitude is also expressed to the Oxford University Press for permission for references from Henry Bettenson, *The later Christian Fathers*, OUP, 1974.

Bernard Lonergan

Note:

I recommend the following excellent introductory works: John Benton, Alessandra Drage, Philip McShane, *Introducing Critical Thinking,* Axial Press, Halifax, Nova Scotia, 2005; Thomas V.Daly S.J., *Learning from Lonergan at Eleven,* in Method: Journal of Lonergan Studies, March 1991,44-63; *What is Metaphysics?* in The Australian Lonergan Workshop II, Novum Organum Press, Drummoyne, Sydney, 2002, 1 7; William J.Danaher, *Insight in Chemistry,* Lanham, Md. USA, University Press of America, 1988; Robert Doran, *Lectures on Insight,* NP3 Discs, 2004: Lonergan Research Institute, Regis College, Toronto; Charles Hefling, *Why Doctrines,* The Lonergan Institute at Boston College Chestnut Hill, Mass, 2000; Richard M Liddy,*Transforming Light:Intellectual Conversion in the Early Lonergan,* Michael Glazier: Collegeville, Minnesota, The Liturgical Press, 1993; Ben F. Meyer, *Critical Realism and the New Testament,* Princeton Theological Monograph Series, Pickwick Publications, Allison Park Pennsylvania, 1989; Hugo A. Meynell, *An Introduction to the Philosophy of Bernard Lonergan,* University of Toronto Press, Toronto,2nd edit. 1991; Matthew Ogilvie, *What is intellectual conversion?* in The Australian Lonergan Workshop II, Novum Organum Press, Drummoyne,Sydney, 2002, 31-47; Neil Ormerod, Bernard Lonergan in *Introducing Contemporary Theologies,* Orbis Books; New York, Maryknoll,2002; Terry J.Tekippe, *What is Lonergan up to in Insight?* A Primer. Michael Glazier, Liturgical Press, Collegeville,1996; Michael Vertin, *Dialectically Opposed Phenomenologies of Knowing: A Pedagogical Elaboration of Basic Ideal Types* in Lonergan Workshop IV. Edited by Fred Lawrence, Chico, California: Scholars Press, 1983, 1-26.

CPSIA information can be obtained
at www.ICGtesting.com
Printed in the USA
LVHW092131131121
702953LV00011B/161